*Southern*
Messenger
Poets

DAVE SMITH, EDITOR

From
a Person
Sitting in
Darkness

new and selected poems

G ERALD B ARRAX

Louisiana State University Press *Baton Rouge* 1998

Designer: Michele Myatt Quinn
Typeface: Granjon
Typesetter: Wilsted & Taylor Publishing Services

Library of Congress Cataloging-in-Publication Data

Barrax, Gerald W.
    From a person sitting in darkness : new and selected poems /
    Gerald Barrax.
        p.   cm. — (Southern messenger poets)
        ISBN 0-8071-2313-7 (cloth : alk. paper). — ISBN 0-8071-2314-5
    (paper : alk. paper)
        I. Title.   II. Series.
    PS3552.A732F76   1998
    811'.54—dc21   98-37901
                                                       CIP

Most of the poems herein have been selected from: *Another Kind of Rain* (University
of Pittsburgh Press, 1970), copyright © 1970 by Gerald Barrax; *An Audience of One*
(University of Georgia Press, 1980), copyright © 1980 by the University of Georgia Press;
The Deaths of Animals and Lesser Gods (Callaloo Poetry Series, 1984), copyright © 1984
by Gerald Barrax; and *Leaning Against the Sun* (University of Arkansas Press, 1992),
copyright © 1992 by Gerald Barrax.
    Grateful acknowledgment is also made to the editors of the following periodicals,
in which some of the new poems, or versions of them, first appeared: *American Poetry
Review, Callaloo, Gettysburg Review, Prairie Schooner, Shenandoah,* and *Southern Review.*

For my mother, father, and brother, dead.
And for Frances Barnes, whose love kept Harold alive.

The Person Sitting in Darkness is almost sure to say, "There is something curious about this—curious and unaccountable. There must be two Americas, one that sets the captive free, and one that takes a once-captive's new freedom away from him, and picks a quarrel with him with nothing to found it on, then kills him to get his land."
—Mark Twain, "To a Person Sitting in Darkness," 1901

From my own point of view, the fact of the Third Reich alone makes obsolete forever any question of Christian superiority, except in technological terms. White people were, and are, astounded by the Holocaust in Germany. They did not know that they could act that way. But I very much doubt whether black people were astounded—at least, in the same way.
—James Baldwin, *The Fire Next Time*, 1963

Contents

I. From *Another Kind of Rain* (1970)

Efficiency Apartment   3

Drought   9

The Scuba Diver Recovers the Body
    of a Drowned Child   10

Five-Part Invention   11

I Called Them Trees   18

Your Eyes Have Their Silence   20

January 16, 1967: 5:30 P.M.   21

Obits   22

Another Way of Dying   24

First Carolina Rain   26

Earthlog I   27

C for Charlie   29

Third Dance Poem   30

Odysseus at the Mast   32

The Quick   33

Fourth Dance Poem   35

The Dozens   36

Earthlog: Final Entry   37

II. From *An Audience of One* (1980)

In the Restaurant   41

King: April 4, 1968   42

The Singer   44

Visit   46

A Means of Travel   47

I Travel with Her   49

She Listens to Madrigals   51

The Fourth Son   53

Something I Know About Her   55

Shani   56

Ghosts   59

Narrative of a Surprising Conversion   60

"I had a terror—since September"   62

Hubris   63

Confession   64

Gift   66

Between Us and the World   67

Another Fellow   68

The Passage of Shiva   69

Ligustrum   71

Black Cat   72

Moby Christ   74

Near the End of a Savage Winter   75

The Buffalo Ghosts   77

An Audience of One   78

III. From *The Deaths of Animals and Lesser Gods* (1984)

The Conception of Goddeath   83

Competitors   85

Barriers   87

More or Less   88

Who Needs No Introduction   89

In This Sign   90

One of My Own   98

Slow Drivers   99

Spirituals, Gospels   101

From a Person Sitting in Darkness   102

One More Word   105

Another Creation   106

To Waste at Trees   107

Symbiosis   108

Poems Like This.   110

Two Figures on Canvas   111

Portraits   112

Recital   113

Lovers   114

Greenhouse   115

All My Live Ones   117

"School Days"   119

If She Sang   120

Dara   121

Liberation   122

God's Button   124

The Death of Another Fellow   126

IV. From *Leaning Against the Sun* (1992)

Eagle. Tiger. Whale.   133

Not Often near Such Water   135

Domestic Tranquility   139

Whose Children Are These?   140

Special Bus   142

Strangers Like Us: Pittsburgh,
    Raleigh, 1945–1985   143

Haunted House   144

Yardwork   146

What More?   149

Two Poems for Miller Williams   151

Epigraphs   152

Sportsfan   157

War Film: Dying Forever   159

Uniforms   161

Adagio   163

Cello Poem   164

V. New Poems

Counting the Ways   175

Sainthood   176

Sunday, 24 May 1992, 10:30 A.M.   177

". . . and tell the girls to pray for me"   178

To My Mother, in Heaven   182

Trio for Two Voices and Bass Clarinet   185

Reunion Birthday Poem
    (With a Line After Cummings)   186

Reunion: Our Common Language   187

The Old Poet Is Taken in Marriage   188

Perfect Stranger   191

The Guilt   192

Jeopardy   193

In Their Heaven   194

Pittsburgh, 1948: The Music Teacher   195

Surreal Dreams: After Watching
    the Discovery Channel   197

Hands Off   199

Helen and the Animals   200

No Answers   201

From *Another Kind of Rain* (1970)

EFFICIENCY APARTMENT

My sons.
sometimes I can / not name you
until this magic room is sleeping,
and the stretched out ends our lives make
curl around
and stitch you through the interstices
behind my eyes.

*

(And ceremonies changed us
And equaled what we became
And ceremonial words preceded us
Into flesh and spirit and aborted us
Into the ends our lives made
With marvelous cadences to tell us what we were
And would be.)

*

One, Two, and Three
when the room is awake and shrugs the shadows off its walls
I see the papered magic I've added
scraps left over from the ends the world made
Roger is jolly on the wall and says Hi
Hippity Hop skips under the breast of a dragon's shadow
        that burns yellow leaves in green flame
The moonmen's marbled earth
        (that I gave your names to remember me)
floats in space above the telephone
And what you drew and gave me once on a visit
        One, your seraped boy with the cactus grin
        Two, your Sopwith Camel firing four lines
                of wavery pencil rounds into the dragon's mouth
                    (I arranged it that way to conserve the forest)

Three's cycloptic snaggletoothed house
I call children's art when visitors ask

*

(Dear, lost, penultimate love
Poorer for, richer for rituals
Of birth and mortgage
We made formality of ceremony
And two or three and ten years
Was too long to live the deaths
That did us part.)

*

Your schoolday weather.

(Did she know the probability of rain?)

Winter mornings close the room.
She wakes you before leaving
and unthreads you from my sleep.

(Did she hear the forecast at all?)

Twelve and $^1/_2$ miles and one river
is close enough to dress you in three warm apologies

for being here.

In bells and voices at noon
in the center of a cross—

church, funeral home and two schools—
it opens   and   I am imprisoned
by the shouting sons of other fathers
playing (

*

Did I play with you?

        (We gave us One for our youth
        Two for love
        Three the image of me.)

Is a father with no sons
a nursery with no rimes
songs, music
now
roses no rings
but ashes   ashes
down the hill we fell
rolling One   sliding Two   tumbling Three

out of the ends of our lives

now

I am black sheep
three boys empty

I will go hi
        (Spy in her eye)
round my base is
round my base
hidingO seekand
daddy's
(find me!)
(lost)
   it

           *

        (I wed thee
        I ring this with what we were
        In seeming real
        One   in

```
Two          seemly
Three        black
             sons.)
```

                    *

Books all over the place

```
my little people     big people
slim and fat         —boys
```

daddy does well in school—

they hunch in bookcase caves
and a box under the table
and squat on top of the closet
in my efficient kitchen
they are a comfort these days
chatting away in my unsleeping
exorcising the square deific

After opening the doors out of your lives
    boys
        I followed the little people leading the piper

and here I am
12$\frac{1}{2}$ miles and one river

            wondering:what if I kill them

will they drown or burn
                        and then?

But no I guess
I have already given my only begotten sons
to save them
            and
every week

it seems
I buy at least one
more

                    *

Hello.   Hello.   Hello.

and to make him laugh I play my old game
            Is that you, Sam?

I have no son by that name.

It was funnier when
they'd come home from
school and I'd keep
them waiting outside the
back door asking who
they were *Is that*
you Sam Harry Joe?
and they'd fall all
over each other shrieking

no daddy
it's *us*!

Hello,Hello.   hello.
what were you doing
how is school
are there grapes on the vine yet
I'll see you soon   I dont know
goodnight goodnight goodnight
no   tell her goodnight for me

                    *

(Even now
The cadence of our changes remains in phase.)

7

I had only to become what I am
And you what you will not.
Hotter than a pepper sprout
I am learning to play the guitar you gave me
Trying not to smoke
So much.
Peace. Your hold forever
            And now speak.)

                    *

Here we go round
here we go round
the Supremes hover above my feet
    the 3 girls I'll never have
the telephone is sorry
the room is raining, efficiently
the room rains and rings
the ends are stitched together
One, Two and Three
                    will be fine
the fit will survive

I have made us all typical
now
true to myself
the nigger daddy of social statistics

(is it asleep?   yes
sleeping and raining and ringing)

goodnight   goodnight   goodnight
Dennis   Jerry   Josh

Drought

This could be the way
the fire comes: God's
fine irony withholding rain.
We could wait for the comfort
of overstatement (half the Flood was tears)
such as something going out of orbit,
falling into the sun
as another kind of rain,
but where is His hand in fire
if the woods are dry?

The woods are dry.
Leaves curl, brown,
fall from God's head
and crackle underfoot like irony's laughter.
At twilight a forest burns
and the sun goes down in more splendor
than even God gave it.
Only I am its match.
My roots need rain, too,
but neither rain nor fire
tells me if it is man or god who is chained to this rock.

The Scuba Diver Recovers the Body of a Drowned Child

Maria, she said. No city river
Should take a name like that.
You should have been an island child and dived or fallen
Into water that liquified sunlight. Once,
        in the Bahamas, Maria, I saw
a school of fish frightened by the shadow of a plane.
There aren't enough Marias
Even in the Caribbean with all its light
To give one of you to this waste and muck.
You must have died in the taste of mills and factories. When
        the shadow passed
over the water I was swimming among them.

How much of your life was there to see
To make you almost forget to breathe?
It was down here, waiting for you. Scenes
Passing out of all our lives into yours. Bright
        sun. The painted fish
swimming in and out of the coral around me.

Your mother said . God, here under the river.
You're a beautiful girl she said.
All our lives have passed. Your black world blacker
Here where the sun never reaches. Next
        summer the sands will be whiter I will go down deeper
without my mask   come up and let the air suck my lungs out

when we go up Maria
she will arrange your hair
and the wind will dry it
sun warms you
she said you were beautiful
she will recognize

FIVE-PART INVENTION

> Keep up your bright swords, for the dew will rust them.
>
> —Shakespeare, *Othello*

I. *Nude as Cassandra*

I didn't need to be Juliet's death-crossed
boy with tragedy possible now for common
men, but the news media chronicle it
with the homage of pity and terror that belongs
to life, as if death were not more common than man.

We had no names to give us immunity
from the colors of our eyes, and only where
we lived made mornings heavy enough with dew
to extinguish burning crosses. Somewhere
among her hills she strummed her guitar,
singing wind, singing rain. I listened, begged her
to come to me, hoping something tragic
for those who let us go, kissed away her
singing with praise and promises, our eyes
on the swords hanging over our heads.

II. *Nude with Apple*

She should expect any fool to flatter her
but didn't know that in her were
countries still virgin to praise. Her sighs
(she knew no better) should have been weary
of apostrophe for her thighs, unmortal
breasts too small for anything but
an abstract like beauty, whose warm faces
budded with praise in far less surprise than hers.
And oh her eyes. Her eyes. Her. Eyes.

III. *Nude with Flowers*

I promised her probable things
I knew were mine to give with less
Certainty than sorrow and love
For her double crossed heart—the heart

That took cavalier promises,
Made them flower and grow terrifically
lavish, even wearing them as
Flowers, visible, her new

Extravagance becoming her so well
She said she thought to say to those
Who saw her disarray and cloud
Of hair as she ran to where I

Was, "I don't care. I'm his girl."
She walked into our rented room
To see and be what I had said.
"Teach me," she said, "not to hurry.

Teach me not to reach and hurry
To try to catch my ringaround
Merrygo. Slow me. Oh slow me."
She came and wrapped me in her

Hasty hair and rubbed me with it
Everywhere to warm my blood
And see if we could teach the terror
Of love to those whose love we praised

For being there. She flowered there,
Remembering promises, made
The room tremble with her waiting—
And oh her eyes. Her eyes. Her. Eyes,

IV. *Nude with Seaweed*

Outside the high room
where the Ohio sprang from two rivers
at the Golden Triangle
      I gave her   made her
      oceans   and   seas
      big enough to drown us
wherever there was white sand
beaches, birds to clap her hands

lovely as she was
the rivers took us from the city's waste
to high air   salt   bright and clean
to break the heart.

I have willingly drowned a little
in bodies of water and women
(once   (when I was younger and believed in words
               they said it wouldn't be over my head
               and I jumped. It wasn't true:
               the blur of all my tall days
               until Eddie's hand like God's
               reached through the blue sky and water
               wedded for my dying.

I know that blood
sounds the same in near death and love
its impact on the organs
before it flows back
but what makes it go there
at all
     God
what makes it not
           flow there?

                  Hero: *My love, will you not drown*
                        For love of me?

[handwritten marginalia: - Rain imagery / - Well-versed in classics]

Leander: *O my lady I try O*
I try!

    Her

body submerged.
Undulating
arched.
And gaping at her the first time
Openmouthed
I should have swallowed and gushed
the ocean itself. I love
you O
I said and she
waited and arched and undulated
in the tower room where we had opened the blinds
to the turning birds
I waded at the edge of the sea
between the white sand and sun.
She thrashed her pillowed thighs
she undulated arched swam
    out there waiting for me
    and I waded little by little, unable to swim into the sea
    hearing her think of promises.
But I love
you (she only waited
hush
    now. Later. There still is time.

        .   .   .   .   .

We lay covered from the dry floor
her softness scissoring me
(soft . think . only flesh)
bedsoft now remembering promises
reading erotica I brought
for the sake of
me   (What is the sound of time waiting in the blood?)
    Keep reading. Keep
    reading. There. Now. Yes

        Isolde: *We sail to my husband.*
        Better we return

14

> *To Ireland or cast our-*
> *selves into the sea.*
> Tristan: *There is no drowning for*
> *me.*
>
> *I will die in sight of you and the sea.*

She
called from the middle
of the water. The sun
sank lower and still
between her and drowning
and me. This time I pulled her out.
With me. I
saved her.

. . . . .

When the sun was gone
there was no sun but her
We brought the moon from the wall
We talked face to face
We held
hoping for catastrophe
flood, tidal wave
on the pillow. We laughed discovering each other as children
growing up. I was a beamish boy.
We grew in minutes to the room.
I love
thee. The silence we stared into.
And my silence poised at the edge of her waiting
    breaking over the crest and falling
        down and closing itself in her . Eyes

> Helen: *Agamemnon will follow us to Troy*
> *Across the wine-dark sea.*
> *There will be death and destruction*
> *Because of you and me.*
> Paris: *The sea is calm.*

The third time under
near death and love
the blood sounds

down again
I sank for her center of gravity
  where I would never be seen
    on the face of the earth in
      any eyes but hers   seeing
        the rest of our lives beyond the room
this time
          the sea in her wedded to our electric moon
I was there
there and touched the bottom of the deepest promise (O
slow me)   the nearest deep to swim or crawl from
              back to land   and yes
Yes she said you
are O and O fuck me and
and
but I couldn't stay,
buoyant, shot up,
fighting the pull of the rocking earth
and busybody tidal moon in the socket by the bed
unable to scream
knowing I would see her
in my life no more
no more
No
coming up through the salt
(I love thee
washed up out of her
eyes

                    Outside that high window
                    gulls flashed white wings
                    in the moonlight
                    turning
                    as her hand turned and curved
                    down into the harbor
                    where the empty boats
                    rocked
                    with the pull of the moon

waiting for morning to put to sea
trailing nets
and swooping birds

V. *Nude with Tumblers*

I had wanted to see you sleeping. We had
Hours and world enough in what little time.
In that high place hours enough to feed and tame
What ravished us. Hours enough to place your head
Within my arm where I could breathe and mouth
Your hasty hair and the sweet proof that the myth
Of your sisters and my brothers (sad
As what it meant for us) was true. Your small
Hand made the random, secure movements of a child,
Sleeping, on my chest. You warm against the cold
Expanse of the room. Against me. I would smell
The warmth of your sleep. Now. Here. After. And what
Ever ritual your waking, I would wait
Out my life for your sleep, and my death to recall.

The hours but not the time for sleep. We lay
In wait like desperate vampires for the smell
Of my blood under the sheets, turgid in the feel
Of your hand. For my own hands I could not destroy
The picture that now provides my private hell.
Nude in motion, smiling, seeing me kneel
As you came from the bathroom with the glasses. I pay
For your picture with my hands and stay
Just ahead of my lust. For thinking I will
Forget goddamn you after all for the fool
I expect to be like any moisteyed boy
Mourning his first love. Those swords in the chill
Morning of our love tarnished by dew as cool
As your eyes, unearned and put away, they
Decay in rusted disuse our every gray day.

I Called Them Trees

The last time
                    I went to the library
I looked at the flowers
surrounding the statue of Steven Collins
Foster and the old darkie ringing
            the banjo at his feet
                                    :flowers planted
in four triangular beds
alternating red and white.
I saw they were all the same kind.

There were others
                        in front of the building
in long wide rectangular rows
bordered by round clusters of pastel green
and white that were too deep, too dark
        red, maroon, for easy images
                                    :I called

them all flowers.
And the stunted trees I
wished I had known, bending over the green

terrace above the flowers
        like women whose faces
I couldn't see washing
their hair in deep green pools, I called
trees. If I had told you would you
        have known them?
                                    There were
flowers for me. There
were trees. There were kinds
of birds and something blue
that crouched
                    in the green day waiting

for evening.
If I had told you would
you have known?

I sat
      on a bench among flowers
and trees facing
the traffic   surveying all

I knew of impalas, cougars, falcons
barracudas, mustangs, wild
                    cats,
marlins, watching cars
go by.   I named them
    all.

Your Eyes Have Their Silence

Your eyes have their silence in giving words
back more beautifully than trees can rain
and give back in swaying the rain
that makes silence mutable and startles nesting birds.

And so it rains. And I speak or not
as your eyes go from silence suddenly
at love to wonder (as those quiet birds suddenly
at rain) letting, finally, myself be taught

silence before your eyes conceding everything
spoken as experience, as love, as reason
enough not to speak of them, and my reason
crawls into the silence of your eyes. Spring

always promises something, sometimes only more
beauty: and so it rains. And I take
whatever promise there is in silence as you take
words as rain and give them back in silence before

there are ways to say that more beauty is nothing
for you before my hands can memorize
the beauty of your slender movements and nothing
is beautiful as words nesting in your eyes.

January 16, 1967: 5:30 P.M.

so that you will know where the sun was
    . Too cold to look up but going downhill
home, I saw the pink contrail, so high

it began the length of my thumb behind
    the silver nail, going somewhere northwest,
just going, like one of the kids running down the street

streaming long crepe paper behind just to keep
    it in the air. "Beautiful," I said,
committing myself, thinking about the

cold up there surrounding the pilot
    in the cockpit, comforted by warm
instruments and dialfaces. Then, more than

I could bear, another, coming from where
    the first was going, their flight patterns
giving them all the margin of safety

from fingertip to elbow, they passed—
    the ductile, malleable cold making
pink parallel bars that showed how pilots

go from where to when, and why horizons
    lose their distance between the points of going.
Forced into a judgment this time, I saw

that it was good and let them go wherever
    they were going, let the sun go down,
and turned the corner home to my own warm faces, and rested.

Obits

1. *Deaths Yesterday*

I was alive yesterday but sleeping late.
The sun rose in the same way
and went straight down the path
behind the column of trees   outside my window

the leaves sucked the light in
breathed oxygen out   burned the morning away.

When I awoke this morning
the paper had printed in columns

the names of those who died after it went to bed
yesterday.

2. *Previous Deaths*

I have been alive since Friday but in my room
studying and writing and didn't see
the weekend. Saturday night the weather
turned cool.

Sunday evening I opened my curtains
and sat looking into the street   through the trees

I saw the sun setting
on a girl walking far

down the street and I loved her.
This morning, Monday,
the paper printed the names
of those who had died over the weekend.

3. *Deaths Elsewhere*

I have been alive but dying
   in helms with crests like blue wheat
      wide-eyed shields   sliding blades   blood, mud
         sacrilege for the earth where no home is,   monoculared

in wheeling vultures, the worship of jackal teeth:
choreography of sudden space, rope-rhythm under the feet

bloodthick,penitent, eyesburst,tongue,penisthrust purged in kerosene:
the suns, the million summers in immolation   suttees   doves

heretics of wood for stakes and chairs   bubbled   crinkled skin:
trials of water   suicide,   flood   gifts of tongues

eyes, bones to the pearls and coral of the sea:
in mushrooms   mushrooms blossoming in my skies

my love   my love   umbrellas c o ∧ e r our lives.

I awoke one morning late   and missed the world,
got the paper and started reading through:
all deadlines made   promises kept   I found it
in sect. 3, p. 4, col. 2.

Another Way of Dying

> The body's judgment is as good as the mind's and the body shrinks
> from annihilation. We get in the habit of living before acquiring the
> habit of thinking. In that race which daily hastens us toward death,
> the body maintains its irreparable lead.
>
> —Camus, *The Myth of Sisyphus*

A whim is all it takes
and there's the race

a rape by the mind
makes shambles of temples
and images
              every day
    nature fills her womb
    with our dead
and blooms

with the elements of all our griefs like a mad girl with flowers.

The fingers and lips as tender as rain
below my belly feel my heart and
feed me the darkest warmest
moments of life.
Only the mind
would call
the turn
the other way
and deny the truth I find when
my own hand turns against me where
the blood goes back and forth
below my belly
        Oh
oh death where are you now?

You neither frighten nor
amuse the rain whose
voices still whisper
mutinies to spring
                who breaks our hearts
more than you
                with the indifference
of her green
              forgiving eyes.

First Carolina Rain

and
so
this is the way
it rains in carolina
23 sept 69
school started for them
in pittsburgh too
and they don't need this kind of rain
especially my second son
the grave serious one
needs dry weather
to carry his busted arm to school
(glad I tried to teach all three
ambi
    dexterity)
need it or not
i carry the rain to school with me
sometimes seeing in students' black faces
my own sons
wondering how it will be to face them
when they reach this age

EARTHLOG I

Our Great Gift. we thought .
Even for Us the error was co
   loss
   all
to make them beautiful
so that beauty would please,
   distract them
   as they grew

They did that.

To the majority we gave correspondences to seasons
skin medleys
color melanges

We were fair with the rest.
All those colors for hair, autumn mostly
the trees   the leaves
   everything complementing them all

  not enough
Things to play with. Baubles.
No more significance than a whim.
Lust of our eyes for variety . color . beauty .

They did.

(Maybe when love is back
in
          fashion
The crew grows weary.
Oh, shit.

There are more alarums among the passengers.
Shiva wants to destroy them all,
now.
J. C. says he will never go back
there.

C FOR CHARLIE

It's a way of keeping informed I guess
but I'm easier to get along with
if I can just get through the day with
out reading a newspaper. It's
the risk I take between Peanuts and Vietnam.
    Charlie Brown has to win a game soon
    for the sake of common decency or no
    body will believe in anything.

What I believe now
is that children would rather play
    in their own shit than with fire
the way Charlie Brown keeps burning them in there
and getting knocked on his ass just because he
    keeps trying.
    But given time enough he may prove himself
a quitter and become a real kid
diddling himself and setting fire to cats
and other innocent small things.

    Do mothers
still hang gold stars in windows
for sons who burned them in there?
    This is known as success.
Patriotic grief is palpable and its taste is good
and Charlie Brown's ERA was out of sight
    anyway.

Third Dance Poem:
In Slow Motion on a Split Screen

> The Greeks were cowardly in their fights, as most wise men are;
> but because they were learned and well taught, they bore their
> sickness with Patience and severity.
> —Jeremy Taylor, *Holy Dying*

The football spirals straight up, rolling from the fingertips
        of the young onearmed
    intramural Greek who
drifts, drifts under it on the green wide campus.
        He is alone in the middle
    of his half of it, of course.
It has to be that way for him and the sake of this poem.

                            On the other half
the young Spartan Chorus moves in one voice
        & speaks in cadence
    through tragic masks
for some of the citizens, older. "You had a good home but you left.
        You're right!" There are
    some angry young Athenians
who don't like it & want them off their half of the screen.
        The Academy is
    no place for this
sort of thing, they protest, & surround the field & pass out
        pamphlets. The one
    armed intramural Greek's
left sleeve is pinned to his shoulder. He doesn't care
        & neither do they,
    who won't look. He drifts
a little & snatches the ball to his side just as it touches
        his fingertips. Sometimes
    he throws or kicks it
away from him & runs his onearmed way to catch it.
        When he misses, he shakes

his head, down, dis-
couraged. He cares about that. What good would a one armed
      Greek have been at
   Thermopylae anyway? (It's the only
battle I know to mention except Hill 871,
      or Olympus, as they called it
   then, where the gods fought.
Let them. We try to bear our sicknesses without complaint
      except in war.
   The Spartans march across
the green grass again with shouldered arms. The Athenians
      roar. The onearmed Greek
   sits on the ground and tries
to tie his shoe. Our childhoods end in frustration.

Odysseus at the Mast

They lashed him halfway up the mast
And he screamed above the silent oarsmen
As they rowed him relentlessly away
From the bone-cluttered island shore of the Sirens
Sitting in the flowers singing unearthly promise.

    They saw the ship go by,
    and the madman raving there.
    One of them stood up,
    still singing, and made gestures
    with her aching body, using
    hands between thighs, showing
    as well as singing.
    The ship went on by wind and oars.
    The voices faded.
    They shrugged, sucked their sharp teeth,
    and went back to their flowers.

His anxious men, blessed with the silence
Of the blind, saw only the soundless agony
As he fought the bonds of the rigid mast
For the vision the Sirens never dreamed
In a world that faded for ever as he moved

Through life after life in the ship at the mast
And his screaming for release, ceased.
They lowered him down among their flesh
And he mastered again his own flesh and his ship
And remembered, once, an impotent whim for mutiny.

THE QUICK

Every day the old Negro moves the sprinkler
about the lawn of the funeral home.
From my window next door I watch it operate.

The mechanical arm trips up and down
interrupting the jet of water, sending
tracers of transparent rounds revolving

over the green green grass, bursting
in crystal flak among the leaves of the small trees
that border the drive. Today

I had to dodge the spray along the sidewalk.
Where the lawn slopes down to the hedges along the walk,
someone had slipped on the grass, so thick,

so green, so wet, their heels had gouged
long furrows in the rich brown
fertilized soil underneath.

                    At night

it's a quarter of a block whiter than anything
on earth. Surrounded by black trees
it blazes in its floodlights and sprouts
green and green awnings at every

window and porch. Nothing goes out
or off all night except the twin
fountains in the corners of its wings
that gush sprays of synchronized red white

violet and yellow until two a.m.
Hung in burning oils inside, more

lifelike than real, the founder
looks out through his long glass-enclosed

entrance and trellised, moss-hung
carport and accepts with benevolent vagueness
my tribute of surprise
each time I walk past at night.

There is a phone booth on the corner a little
past where I turn in. On a quiet night
I could hear if it ever
                    rang

Fourth Dance Poem

In legend, the appearance of White Ladies usually forebodes
death. In Normandy they lurk on bridges and other narrow
places and ask the traveler to dance. If he refuses the Lady he is
thrown into a ditch.

The White Lady has asked me to dance.
She had been lurking under the bridge I had to cross
   to go anywhere.
I've considered my answer
and since I've stopped denying it
                   she knows I have natural rhythm
so will she believe I don't know this dance?

"Why dance we not? Why stand we still?"

She has seen the white feather
I wear in my cap like a plume
and doubts my honesty
but I say to her anyway
ah White Lady
but I don't know this dance.

She hasn't believed me.

"They flee from me that sometime did me seek."

Oh White Lady
now you've said it

for me it was a long walk from Alabama

and I was on my way anywhere

The Dozens

A Small Drama in One Act, One Scene

Big Boy   (Sophisticated, worldly-wise with the knowledge
                   learned from listening to the hip talk of other Big Boys):

                   Yo momma yo momma yo momma
                   yo mom ahhh yo maaa yo mommmmmmmmUHma
                   momma yo yo mommamommamomm
                   ahhhhhh yo momma yoooOOOOOHHHH MAN
                   yo MOMMA!

Little Boy   (The Innocent who hasn't heard the hip talk of the Big
                   Boys. He doesn't understand why there are tears in his
                   eyes, but he knows, vaguely, that he must reply):

                   An' ... an' ... and you is ANOTHER one!

EARTHLOG: FINAL ENTRY

Early in the voyage
we discovered idolatry among the passengers.
We tried to let them alone because we thought they needed it
but it's a small ship
and even with our guidance system its course through Chaos
had been erratic
and they threatened destruction   in our names
though there was no jealousy among us.

We let them act out
their ceremonies and rituals to us
in the name of the names they called us
                     and they died in each other's arms
"honkies niggas papists kikes wops mohammedans"
died on the altars in their minds
                 snarling eyes
                 fists locked
                 on crosses, manifestos, texts they called "sacred"

We wept
and comforted each other
                 when they tore out the hearts of their sons
                 to please us
ashamed to be prophets and gods to fools

Now the sons of devils and slaves watch the stars
and navigate well
and call themselves "Men."

It's a relief to feel not needed.
         Our deaths or retirements
         may be imminent

II

From *An Audience of One* (1980)

In the Restaurant

I understand
Watching this public exposure
Of mere flesh that must be fed

Why I must keep away
From the tables of my enemies
Or lose them.

Poor creatures
Betrayed by this ritual
They don't know how vulnerable we are

When their heads go down
To meet their forks
It's a gesture too much like prayer

A cry for help, a plea for kinship.
Whether something else's predator or my own enemy
Dripping the blood of a warm kill

Between the jaws of either
Death holds us closer than hate
Feeding us mortality in such small portions.

KING: APRIL 4, 1968

For Eva Ray

When I was a child
in the Fall the axes fell
in Alabama and I tried
to be somewhere else,
but the squeals of the pigs dying
and hogs and the sight of their
opened throats were everywhere .

I wasn't given that kind of stomach.

When I was 14, I killed
my last thing bigger than a mouse
with my Daisy Red Ryder,
a fat robin on a telephone wire,
still singing,
as my first shot went high
I sighted down and heard from where I was
the soft thud of the copper pellet in his
fat red breast. It just stopped
and fell over backwards
and I had run away
before it hit the ground, taking
my stomach with me.

I'll never know about people—
if the soft thing in the stomach can be cut out—
because I missed all the wars—
but when I learned that non
violence kills you anyway
I wished
I wished I could do it I wished I
could
do you know what it means to wish

you could kill to
wish you were given that?

But I am
me. Whatever made me made
you, and I anesthetize the soft thing
to stop squirming when
you do it brothers I shout
righton righton rightON
my heart is with you
though my stomach is still in Alabama pig
pens.

THE SINGER

For Sarah, Nina, Roberta,
Aretha, Ella, Carmen.
Dinah, Billie, Bessie. And Ma.

Black Angel
Doing what she's gotta do
The sister sings

"Like a stone bird"
He said, intending to praise her.
But no bird has such a choice.

They speak too,
Or whatever twittering means
But does that explain human song?

Maybe this more than natural impulse
Surprised even the creator
Who had let the possibility

Slip his mind.
Not unintended.
Just not thought of.

       Suppose
there was a creature
not yet human
Who cocked his head, dimly quizzical
at birdsong
and did something—
roared screeched, howled—
something purely joyous in imitation
and those birds filled the prehistoric air
in flight from his obscenity.
Who was to tell him

he wasn't created for that? Or
suppose Eve.
Giving a name
to something dull Adam
didn't know about:
What's that? What are you doing?

And she, holding the doomed child
stopped and looked at him as if listening
and smiled, and said

Singing.

Not like birds
Who are doomed to sing
Her doom and ours is her silence.
Doing what they've gotta do
Black Angels
The sisters sing

VISIT

She holds to the idea
of a husband and three sons.
The accomplishment of it.
My three years away
she holds as hostages
and we move and place each other in cities
whose names become the bonds that hold us.
    Eventually I must go from Durham to Clarksburg,
        the days on Eldora Place
        like the memory of childhood, or water,
            the mortgage and park deceiving us with permanence
            into playing house with real kids.

After eight months
I am saddened that sons can grow so tall
in the absence of their father.

Sunday evening we fished in Buffalo Lake
and I discovered that a father must not think of the worm
when baiting a hook for a son
and little Blue Gills must be killed outright
if they swallow it.
Cold blooded things,
what must a daddy do
when his youngest son brings a fish
hooked through the head and one eye
but pull it out.
It's a sport
and I believe it's said
they feel no pain.
They bleed, but feel no pain.

A Means of Travel

I got to 17 with all my parts
when tonsils were cheap enough
for parents to excuse themselves for sickly sons.
So mine came out.
As long as I was there
I decided to give up that piece of flesh
I was more familiar with.
            (a footnote here
            would expose my precocious ignorance
            in my envy of the skinless boys in the school pool,
            once believing they knew something
            useless for me to lie about—
            that foreskins somehow disappeared into
            or were snatched away by
            whatever girls had that I hadn't.
            But by 17 I'd had my books
            in plain brown wrappers under the mattress
            and knew better, but not much)

Home from the hospital
and just about to graduate,
the girl with whom I'd practiced
kissing to death
gave me a poem.
It was for my throat
(she knowing only half of what I'd lost).
            I was impressed.
And being too sore anyway
in more places than one
to even ask for more,
I wrote one back to her.

Ellen,
whatever has become of you,

I thank you for teaching me
to sublimate the discomfort of my throat
and the agony of my stitched and bandaged dick
into a means of travel.

I Travel with Her

1. *How we look*

Traveling with her
between marriages I found
was a way of picturing things lost
back into my life.
I do it each year on the exact dates, or between,
by slipping into the photos
that show where I've been.

In disguise the first year,
apprehensive about names and hotel registers
in Paris and London we appear
together only three times,
not even chancing
passing friendly natives:
once using the timer I got us lying across the bed
in the Hotel du Mont Blanc studying the map
for the next day's pictures;
and twice at Stratford
where we met Jan,
someone from home who knew too little about the Polaroid
to be afraid to use mine.
Otherwise, the two of us look out at me—
the camera, each, separate, alone.

2. *What we saw*

All the expected sights are there
(count them:name them one by one)
but I felt uneasy about what I didn't get.

On our second morning in Paris
she was awakened at seven

by a girl singing *Santa Lucia* in the street below
accompanied by someone on a violin.
She supposed they were from the Sorbonne
just down the street.
Imagine that happening anywhere back home,
we mused, when I awoke.

   A year later she was home in the Caribbean,
ten years gone, with me along.
This time we both heard the flute,
terrifying her,
at first looking and mistakenly recognizing Brown,
the ghost of her girlhood
who had smelled or heard Death
from whatever island he hobbled on his goat foot
to hang back at the ends of funeral processions.
He had always played, she said, *Abide with Me*.
Shades of Black Pan, then and now.
But not Brown this Sunday. This time a blind one
with a boy outside,
the flute weird wailing
hymns for alms.
      I didn't look out,
      I have no pictures of it,
      so as in Paris I don't know for myself.

   But I know
the danger of being too often behind the lens,
too often not having proof of myself;
I know the possibilities of traveling
in the wrong direction
the opposite way
with my camera empty
maybe never getting back.

She Listens to Madrigals

Take, O take those lips away
That so sweetly were forsworn

Old sweat, the sun, perfume.

The lances dip toward her.
She favors one
But she knows her Freud
As well as any
And closes her legs
Tighter.

The lute plays on her dreaming.

She is assaulted by color,
Livery and armor
Sunstruck in cinerama.
The pennants flutter. She hears
The flourish of long trumpets
Behind the intricate voices.
Fa la la.

. . . those eyes, the break of day,
Lights that do mislead the morn

The sun. Hooves tear up the green turf.
She itches and crawls beneath the colors.
She has not bathed either
To make it as real as she knows it was.

The lutes play on her dreaming.

The lances gallop toward each other
And her favor ripples from the tip of the Black Knight's.
She closes her legs tighter.

But my kisses bring again, bring again,
Seals of love, but sealed in vain, sealed in vain

Her perfect lover, perfect in love, perfect in time
Bows over her hand.
His hair crawls. She holds her breath.
    Smile.
She knows the code demands no more
But is assaulted by hope

As the lances splinter on her symbols of the sun:
The white, the black. The dead wood flowers
Into roses. Her thighs
Part, she has returned.
Take O take those lips away.

The Fourth Son

Halfway through my life I've lived one quarter
to create the persistence of memory
in my memory of the rest. More and
more I lose my place, being lulled

offguard as a sleepy reader: I blink
and discover between period and
capital that some part of my life has
flashed and gone—or that I've been somewhere and back.

I'm always most unprepared for my sons.
They flicker in and out in the random
stages of growth arrested for the rest
of my life by the six years between us

    today. I carry four-year-old Josh
    in one arm to preschool because it was
    so cold and I want to get them there fast;
    fathers sometimes need excuses to hold
    the warmth they love, I never did; Jerry
    I pull along with the other hand, such
    long legs to be only six, was Dennis
    on school patrol? yes Dennis the missing
    son has left early for school patrol. When

I'm back on the page *this time I know*
why you've come: today my new wife

was told that the child we carried
to the hospital two weeks ago
in the plastic bowl proved under the
microscope to have been a perfect

boy, naturally. This time then you'd come for the son that would've been half your brother. We hadn't told you. When you visit next summer, I don't know if we will.

SOMETHING I KNOW ABOUT HER

She touches when she talks—
must touch to smooth out syntax with her fingertips,
must lay on her hand to hear her echo,
to feel the words you don't speak
below the ones you do.

What she means by it is
if she touches you, listen:
to surprise her at it
   would be like waking a sleepwalker
   between two dreams—
would trap her in this tedious
world of mere
         jive
           words.

SHANI

1

Your miraculous conception
was too improbable to be doubted,
to be anything but a human
success: to the very day
following the seven barren years,
to the very April that second-named you
when your mother and I,
naked in the innocence of others' lives,
walked a dying afternoon through a greenhouse.
Whatever there was among those exotic flowers
that yessed us got into her
and drove her
                        life and will
towards you, seven Decembers away.

2

We had expected you
the year before.
A boy came. We grieved for him,
losing the struggle to out-
grow the benign tumors,
the weeds choking him
out, flayed plum.
Her womb made whole again
they took you, without labor,
on the afternoon your mother timed
to end the next year.
                        Three generations of sons
had kept watch for you,
but waiting with the stubbornness of your sign,

you took your own and the world's
sweet time to be born a woman.

3

Halfway through your blind swim
toward us, deeper than need for reason,
you made for my hand at that living wall,
touched it once,
and the half-playful certainty I gave your mother
became real for me. We chose the name, then, for her,
whose need for you exceeded denial,
whose belief had resigned her to sons:
Shani: the wonder, the surprise, the start-
ling event.

4

From under the ocean
where the slave ships once drove
between cold England and St. Vincent
your mother's parents bequeathed you
the sea changes of your Caribbean heritage.
On her side,
on that green Gem of the Antilles
that glows on your wall,
daughters are no less rare
for not being so.

    All through the North
your paternal kin remained exiled
in winter and cities,
still the alien places
long after the Great Migration
from the black soil of our origins.

They waited for word of you.
It had to be here, Home
where December goes out green,
in this South where the last daughter was born.

You arrived as you did,
the year ended, the next began
as if none of you intended
to ever hear of winter again.

5

When I was told they almost severed
the cord that bled you both
I thought of the boy who wouldn't have been you—
  whose pain ended last year
  that wouldn't be yours—
and of my three living sons in that first life before death
lost in the ruins of a marriage
and whose loss is you
and will always be yours.

The burden of each day's guilt
is to deny or balance
the claims of our confusions.
Between the green winters of this second life
and the fatherless profit and loss of the last,
which is the weight,
which the counterweight?

  The distant brothers
 come for 30 days a year
to make us whole again.

GHOSTS

Young and talented, they were so good
With words they had lines to throw away,
Or they sang and he made any stringed instrument
Do clever things behind, under, or around
Her voice. Their best
Was a thing on death that made it
A kind of fool: they loved each other
So much.
          When he started losing her
It was one room at a time
After she'd been the first to learn.
She'd watched and felt the rooms changing
Watched her knees unflex
And when her thighs sank below her own horizon
And she saw what he was doing
There, the look turned both their bodies to stone and salt.
          To be able to let her go
He had to follow her back
Through all the rooms she'd been dying in
And dream she was dead. He dreamed it.
He wrote and sang songs for himself
That would've moved stones or
Death itself if she had been dead.
Then she let him let her go, resurrected
From that house because in everything
They had said whether very clever or merely true
Each would've given back the other's life
To become a stranger in someone else's.
          At first he marveled to be still alive until
He walked from room to room in that house
Afraid to ever look back
And learned that death is less than half of dying.

Guidance counselors at the liberal
integrated northern high school
told the boy after taking written
aptitude tests
that they showed
how good he was with his hands.
That something like carpentry
or auto mechanics
was what he was for.
    He was amazed.
    How could they tell?
    How could they know? He decided then that
white folks must know everything.
He'd wanted to be a pharmacist a lawyer an
engineer a writer a doctor ETC but
none of these
needed the kind of manual dexterity he
never knew he
had, and since they knew
better, he knew in his
awe it was no use. Instead then of
worrying about college any more
and medicine engineering writing ETC he used his hands to
deal, to steal, ETC, i.e., to survive. And when the time
came, instead of being
uselessly out of the way in an
office a classroom on a
bridge ETC when the time came
he was there—
when it was spring or summer on green maps
and somewhere melons were bursting red meat into the sun,
on his block it was the uncertain season
between the cold trickle of black rivulets into gutters
and the slap of the sun's red palm on concrete—

then his long supple black hands curved around the rifle
and the finger lifted from his life
and curved around and oh gently squeezed
and the top of a silky head novaed into the red sun.
Then it knew everything.

"I HAD A TERROR — SINCE SEPTEMBER"

First a terror of choice, but that was done
By September—Renunciation my chosen word.
I hope she knows the troubles, what pools I wade,
What an old romantic ass I've become—
To remember each stage of that delirium,
I bought the albums and use the music we heard
To keep us in time together out of handmade
Memories of loving and scrooving in double-tongue.
Double-stopped now, it's all I can do to hum
The tunes and hang on to what I can, less
Each September, channeling raw music into the wound—
Afraid when she appears in the room
As out of time as music from all this sound
I might say yes this time goddamn I'd say yes.

HUBRIS

As if powered by her bumper stickers,
"I Found It" on one side
and on the right, "This is a God
                    Squad Car,"
CB antenna on top and going
like an angel out of hell, she left behind
this sinner driving Oh so carefully
with his buckled-in daughter
in the 25 miles-per-hour zone.

Confession

They tapped your spine
When you were two
And the microscope showed bacteria in
The fluid—a surprise: your
Symptoms suggested only
A virus. But they'd keep you
To see if a culture grew, just
To be sure. Your mother swayed.
She never left you the next four days
While you lay with the tube they'd looked
Everywhere to find a vein for.

That first night she prayed for
The miracle. At home
I called your grandmother
Up North. She too said she'd pray
For you and told me to
Do the same. I said yes
And stayed awake a long
Time deciding not to and
Reading. I hadn't before.
How could I begin with something
So important as an only daughter?
Shani, two prayers and maybe more
Went out or
Up, but not mine in a night
Whose horror was equal to its
Chance of being you and not
Some other whose recovery might not be better than death.
A martini puts me to sleep when nothing will.

The next day there was a miracle. But the next day
Out mothers
Were no longer believing in or needing
Miracles: they knew

What it was. I said nothing.
But when you came home
Free of the tube and bottle
I first knew the danger of ruining you
For life. All it takes
Is to remember you there
And no matter what you do
It will never be the same
Because God one night
Happened to have been a
Lab Technician who left a careless
Thumbprint on a glass slide.

GIFT

What does it mean
that there is a snake lying among the wild strawberries;
    Spring has laid smooth stones at the edge of the pool;
    there are birds who see farther at night
        than the warm things under cover of purple leaves?
Some god has bitten this mottled apple.
We swim in these summer days, its juices.
What does it matter where the snake hides:
      I was out of place until a blue jay
      in return for my seed
      left that black banded feather from his wing
      in my back yard.

Between Us and the World

The heart relaxes one beat
and dark rain cools the rough skin,
breathing eases,
lungs, needles, and leaves
go out and into the air, ex-
changing molecules between us and the world,
the power in that one light
moves live substances through our systems
like creatures beneath surface tension,
corpuscles oxygenating the sap,
the tingling of photocells
synthesizing sunlight in the blood
to feed the root systems out of the heart
and send the love in the bowels
up the shaft of that power
to these leaves flaming their tips
out into air again.
In the systole
My blood is driven from the chambers of the heart
And extinguishes the fire. My breath withers
The leaves. A thought blasts the roots
From the earth; and the trees howl at the return
Of consciousness and the darkness that was, before
The rain.

ANOTHER FELLOW

The almost whole skin
Lay right outside the window of my basement
Where I'd been entombed for more than a year.
Whenever it happened, if I had raised myself
And looked out of the groundlevel window
I'd have seen it crawling out of its year-old skin;
It would've seen a face marveling and envious
Up from a book behind the screen.
It would've been too busy
Doing what it was supposed to do
To bother with me.
My ancestors, considering its immortality,
Would've welcomed it with food and drink
When it came as spirit of the living-dead from the forest
To visit their huts;
And I would've sacrificed a book to its wisdom
In return for a poem.
   Dear Emily,
That was in September, months ago.
The grass after days of rain was high, wet, still growing
And had to be cut once more for the year. I cut it
In anticipation, wondering if I would drive him
Into the square of the yard, or out,
Half dreading both but needing
One or the other. This year I will be 43.
I found neither the spotted shaft in the high grass
Nor in my room your worm transformed
And ringed with power. I found an empty skin
That I threw over the fence.

The Passage of Shiva

Usually I make better time at night
but starting out at 3 a.m.
there's no place as dark as North Carolina
driving 501 north to West Virginia
black as the inside of a ( )
it's their element,
things crossing the road
unnerving me to slow down:
the prey and predators not knowing the roads say
the world is no longer theirs.

Even cats, who know us so well
      we hate them for their stealth,
when they come to our roads cross them
as blindly as they were built

and I discovered about myself
that I have as much dread of running down
one of those hotly pursuing or pursued
as a man.
          And I did.
Leaping into the lights,
somebody's dog after nobody's rabbit
I hit in midstride, one bite away.

What apocalypse did I bring?
Surely for the prey it was a visitation—
a nova of deliverance:
some passing god or Urban Historian
who saw and rendered immediate justice at 60 mph.
For the dog, the death of a hunter,
the Great Hunter's terrible swift wheels
sending him to eternal good hunting
where the scent was "for ever warm
and still to be enjoyed."

A rationalization, perhaps,
but the road was mine anyway. Ours.

Coming back
I drove all day
when the burrows are carpeted with fur
and cats lie under porches
dreaming of cool and bountiful nights.

LIGUSTRUM

A red spider, delicate, is traveling from the sun
Down the shadows of the Ligustrum.
One branch stirs against the screen,
Nudging October through my window.
    "Hardy hedge plant of the olive family,
    cultivated as an ornamental."
Red spider, travel down into the shadows.
Play,children. Bark,dogs. October
Day,sing.
    "Some varieties have persistent
    semi-evergreen foliage" . . .

    . . . it does feel that way—
Those delicate feet skating
My waxy surface:
And that wasn't just the *wind* pushing my screen . . .

It's more than the wind, or October—that presence
Nodding welcome in the next leaf . . .
    "The oval or oblong leaves are about
    one to one and one half inches long."
No: it's the whole bush and the wind
Going through. "In early summer" we had white flower
Clusters, then the black berries.
    Kids, birds, spider: I have all these nerves
    now to feel you walking delicate feet
    and shouting October through the leaves,
    more ears than the wind.
"Native to northern China. Amur Privet, also called
    Amur River Privet."

    The spider on its way down the bush
    from time to time goes to the tip of a leaf
    and waves half its body and legs out into the sun.
We don't know why it does that.

Black Cat

We saw it sliding into the earth
through an open sewer—
slinking, she called it
with her ordinary distaste for cats.
But it slid down,
the tip of a black tongue
sucked back through iron lips.

I was there two days later
two blocks away, when something
poked the tongue back into light
through the asphalt mask
pressed upon the earth.
It half emerged and saw me
and we looked at each other
for as long as it commanded—
me frozen with one hand
on the car door handle,
it resting half in
half out of the earth,
more than half sphinx
less than half mortal.
It was early morning
and I had been tricked into belief
in eternal sunrise,
but this creature must have been there
        before this sun
when all eyes were yellow-green
less for looking away from light
than into darkness—
when only such eyes were needed
to distinguish beast from man,
the hunter from the killer.

Something flickered back into the green-yellow eyes
and dismissed me back into my sun
to my own destruction
beyond the need of hunting
through the long passages under the foundations
we live on.

Moby Christ

Again, Father,
I've tried to escape the tyranny of your right hand—
how many times among those fools who never know me
until it's too late
and now as lord of these hosts of the waters.

Again, Father,
you've searched me out—
once Judas
and now the divine madness of an old man
to hound me down to the sea like an animal.

My scars multiply:
you'll fill my skin with harpoons
as you've filled my memory with your crosses—
what I must pay
to put spirit into flesh,
to feel, God, to feel
even the pain.
You are old, Father,
a fond and foolish old man
who has never known that much
about what you've created.

My hosts will pay, too.
Men believe I once died for their sins
and now these great creatures will die for mine.
There go the ships, Father,
on your wide sea which your wanton boys
will wash in Leviathan's blood
and hunt down to extinction.

When the sea gives up its dead
Father
will nothing rise from its depths
but the fools who have crawled over the earth?

Near the End of a Savage Winter

In the beginning
winter came disguised in hesitation
and hung back from the blaze of autumn
into the mild year's end
when we celebrated an arbitrary birthday,
still needing something not there
and impatient children
went sledding down the pure white hills
imagined on livingroom carpets.

Their redemption came with the first snow
and ours
when the temperature dropped
and the cold
separated us from memory,
probed white fingers
into our bellies and minds,
found them full
and suitably lulled
by the ways of the world.

Now in the midst of our hungers
we wait in perfect faith for
spring   believing
its coming is inevitable
every year, every year. Every year.

But what lies under the snow
proves that what we have done
is not to be done
for each year the wounds deepen
the channels thicken with waste
and healing becomes more difficult.

We could not survive such cold.
The one eye of the sun.

The one eye of the moon.
The one eye of winter
: these malignant Cyclops have watched us
make the easy acceptances between lion and lamb
too long.
We wait for March and transition,
salvation in the lamb,
but we can not survive such cold
                    and ice hangs under the rocky hillsides
                    as opaque as frozen salt
                    smooth as bands of muscle in a giant's thigh
and, curbed by the sidewalks,
lies uncoiled in black humps along the gutters.

THE BUFFALO GHOSTS

In black windows
Buffalo ghosts are eating the sweet grass
Growing in all the alleys
And main streets of the world.

An Audience of One

It's all so friendly
the way the night is shrieking
a joyful noise unto itself.

My area light is a baton
against the green that's too brilliant,
and the absolute-black interstices of the wall of trees,
all in their perfect places: willows on the left,
oak to the right, maple, pine, and dogwood
orchestrated between, all leaning hungrily toward it,
swallowing the light
that goes into the woods and never
out again.
In there the hunger rages,
so close to my domicile,
things in combat to devour
one another, not at all
the way lovers do.

As an audience of one
it must be me to cough
and applaud the crickets, tree frogs,
and God knows what else
out there.
And I'm discovered.
Monitored,
I'm a terminal whose readouts are taken
and my internal processes fed back into the dark
where it is computed that you are gone from me,
in another part of that world.

Nothing stops completely.
not even the sanest music,

but in sympathy that great heartbeat slows down
and there is a diminuendo in the dark
while the trees and I lean toward
that cool artificial light
as though it were you or the sun.

From *The Deaths of Animals
and Lesser Gods* (1984)

The Conception of Goddeath

The word *forever* would have pleased Him because
He had no name to give the time He had lived,
Each day repeating its unvarying gold.
He knew later that the seasons had not come
Until fear cost Him the sun, but had no memory
Of when the days began, no reason to think
Of their end until He saw His animals dying.
Sparrow Hawk dropped from the sky and stiffened
On the ground. Blue Gill and Mud Minnow turned over,
Bloated in the water. Great Reptiles rotted,
Swelled in the sun. Tiger's yawn locked open,
Her serene eyes gone.
　　　　　　　　He was puzzled, having
Willed none of it. It went on for another
Time of *forever* until the unthinking moment
Inside the Woman, when with a surprised
New gesture, She touched His face. She touched His face,
Became rigid, violent, muscles pulling Him, in waves.
He heard Their breath come back, saw Her eyes close,
And dawn never came more slowly than they
Opened into His ignorance. He had no
Name for what He saw, but His mind exploded,
Awake, memory ticking Him away
From ease, from peace, from fable and light. He tried
The clumsy thought *truth*.
　　　　　　　　　　　He saw in Her eyes
All the blazing days of His life; She, too,
Had always been there; if He turned from Her
He could see nothing. His hand, with the same grace
As Hers, touched Her face. Her eyes closed again.
He began seeing through them and remembered
A beast He'd come across, with ribs like Hers,
But the flesh melting away into the same
Earth on which She lay, the intense Violet,
Anemone, Foxglove, Flame Flower, Lotus,

The darkest Grass growing in the white cage.
The first time now the sunlight rained, burning
His throat. He could not see Her. She shimmered away,
Returned in the raining light. The thing inside
Her burst, exploded backwards into His groin,
Searing inside Him up through His burning
Throat. He swallowed that light, raining, the first
Sound that love made.
                              Wildebeest, Gazelle,
And Unicorn lifted their heads from grazing.
At the second cry they fled, wheeled back and gazed
At the fear. In his mind, from the ground, the air, the first
Word of the god created answered him.
He closed his eyes to fable, tried *truth* again.
Phoenix lighted its first fire. No more
Than a stone's throw away in time Odin, Zeus,
Jehovah, Kali, Allah, the Tezcatlipocas,
Shango also awoke with no memory
Before that cry of human, divine need.

COMPETITORS

We still call it a mother
and taken without love or care
she bears the weight of our faults,
in her huge orgasms grinding her teeth along her own faults
and shaking our buildings down.
If we counted her bodies and our own
we'd see how little help she needs.
But we do help
with engines invented by cunning men
   catapult, ballista, springal, trebuchet
   throwing swarms of arrows spears stones
   crossbows and Greek fire
to do to flesh what they will.
   At that she sighs in another ecstasy
and turns her winds to widow's work
blowing our buildings down,
knowing we have our own ways to help her
with devilish devices invented by disinterested men
   gunpowder, cannon, mortar, rocket
   aircraft, bomb
to do to flesh what they will.
We help celebrate her five million years dying,
old before her time, logrolling her under our feet,
counting our enemies off the other side,
our enemies counting on time to catch up.
   But it keeps its lead
the thing we call a mother.
It turns to the moon
her prodigal lover
back again for her periods of unease
cleansing out her womb with tides that smash down
all we can build or be.
   In spite of all our needs
we help at her labors.
We deliver bodies to fertilize the body we fight over.

We die to make bodies count for something,
to control the places of slaughter
                    that the old terror we still call Mother
                    in the earth wind and water
                    intended as fields of praise.

Barriers

I go out for the news this morning
and find what's left of the slaughtered bird,
guts and wings, on my walk.
I know what did this.
There is someone's black and white cat
that hunts the woods back of our house,
stalking beyond the fence and stealing
some of my admiration for its great cousins
who bring down prey twice their size;
or it perches on a stump
that's a throne among the weeds, a power
in its dominion, so visible
I'd wondered if it ever made a kill.
Now here's the proof at my feet
in these black and white wings.
Today I take my stand against relativists
who reduce moral questions to shades of gray.
Things like this belong in the woods,
and that creature had no right to bring its savagery
across the fence and leave it at my door.
I sweep the thing into the grass
before pregnant Helen sees it.
The ants have already started arriving.
It all bothers my stomach at first, but it helps
to see it as a little chicken.
Like the kind we sometimes dress for dinner.

More and Less

Survivors of war
know best the repeated numb perplexity
that follows grenade explosions within someone else's range;
or the thousand aimless rounds
that people their civilian sleep
with squad after squad of bodies taking someone else's
last step.

But bewilderment follows everyone through fire,
head-ons, hurricane, structural collapse
with the "Why" after the prayer of thanks
or rage against our choice of deities
for the someone who didn't survive.

Except for ego
or some genetic or learned need
to believe in the design of sparrows falling,
we might answer with the *uncertainty* of human events,
stumbling around the nucleus of death
like electrons in unpredictable orbits
of probable place, speed, energy;
like this one leaf falling from autumn today
before another.
Why your race, color, nationality?
Why born? in *1933* and not? when?

When decay or catastrophe collapses all events
into the waiting center,
the single human stake is high enough
to flush minds and hearts free of doubt,

offering the final choice
to pray or curse—if the last ironic flash
shows that chance has played god with the universe.

WHO NEEDS NO INTRODUCTION

Sometimes in the cool of the garden
he walks through the setting that was
his early and, some say, only
success; the birds, flowers, animals
and all the rest whose names he can't
always remember still here,
properties for another try. He picks,
examines a strawberry in amazement, watches
the way the sun comes and goes,
the seasons of the moon. He thinks they
serve him better than the myriad little
theaters that sprang up like weeds
in old gardens, that put on
those amateurish spectacles in his name.
The rivalry between them was killing—each
company with its prescribed repertory of roles,
masks, rituals—none of it adding
to his stature. It was all so wearying.

                    Bursting out of the dew
he loafs with snails under the leaves,
admiring the warm sound their moist
muscles make as they go; or listens
in disbelief to a mad mockingbird,
unable to recall the sanity or the whim
in which he had done that. He imagines
that he had stopped there the first time,
and leans against the grass
in the spot light of his last star.

In This Sign

> He who conquers, I will make him a pillar in the temple
> of my God . . .
>
> —Revelation 3:12

There was no god but Allah
    and Mohammed was his Prophet
There was no god but God
    and Jesus was his Son
There was no god but Gold
    and Europe was its Slave
There was no god for the Slave

I

It was already too late for us
When Simon the Cyrenian was seized
And made the first to feel the weight
Of that Man of Sorrows, who shaped the world
To the four corners of his cross.
Then Constantine's sign of conquest finished us.
Born too soon to know the smell of kerosene,
He saw it wrapped in burlap,
Blazing in the sky, on our hills and lawns,
Illuminating the ghastly black things slaughtered on trees.

II

i. Prince Henry's men come down our coast,
Out to prove the roundness of their world.

    We know ours is, have no reason to explore.
    Its circle is the death of ancestors
    Who watch over us from the forests,
    Their births from them and back again.

But Gonzales comes in 1441, finds us and takes Twelve
Away to Portugal. Not enough.
Never enough. They return in three years.

>"And at last our Lord God
>who giveth a reward for every good deed,
>willed that for the toil they had undergone
>in his service, they should that day obtain victory
>over their enemies, as well as a guerdon
>and a payment for all their labor and expense;
>for they took captive of those moors,
>what with men, women and children, 165,
>besides those that perished and were killed."

Baptisms: 165 washed in the blood of the Lamb
Slaves: 165 washed in the blood of the Lamb.

ii. In 1481 our sphincters tighten for trouble again.
On the Gold Coast, d'Azambuja tells us
They will build a place of worship at Elmina
To bring us their Lord's blessing.

>*Do, Lord, oh do Lord,*
>*Oh do remember me!*

We agree. One can never have too many gods,
We thought, when others had come with crescent and sword
And the gift of Allah.
Some accepted. There were allowed to live—
As brothers, we were told; brothers taken away
Beyond the Great Desert; brothers
We never see again. Our fathers who art.
Spitting in the face of memory,
We agree to this new god.
They put up their place of worship.

They build a fort, they raise a flag, we hear a mass.

III

i. Enter Columbus, declaiming,
>"God has reserved for the Spanish monarchs,

not only all the treasure of the New World
but a still greater treasure of inestimable value,
in the infinite number of souls destined to be brought
over into the bosom on the Christian Church."
Then the Lamb speaks as a Bull from Rome,
And East and West are torn apart
On the horns of an Iberian dilemma.
Pope Alexander says that Spain shall not enter
Africa and encroach upon Portugal.
Spain shall have
the *Asiento* and the rest of the world.
The rest of the world is yellow and black gold.
Gold everywhere they look.
They sweep through the Caribbean,
First falling on their knees
On the groin of the green earth, to pray,
Then on the Indians,
Columbus calls them.
But even that god won't put the gold into their hands.
Somebody must dig it out.
Columbus calls them Indians. They decline,
They escape to the mountains,
Die of Christian diseases,
Die fighting with arrows against steel,
Hunted down, like Indians.
On Hispaniola
Carib Chief Hatuey
is brought to the stake
before a good Franciscan friar.

"My son, do not expose your soul to damnation.
Accept Christ as your Savior that you may find
forgiveness for your sins, salvation, and the blessings
of Paradise."

This Paradise. There are Spaniards there?

"Yes, my son. But only good ones. Only those
who have lived by his Word."

Light your fire.

Ferdinand speaks in Spanish:
> "In view of our earnest desire for the conversion
> of the Indians to our Holy Catholic Faith,
> and seeing that, if persons subject in the Faith
> were there, such conversion might be impeded,
> we cannot consent to the immigration of Moors,
> heretics, Jews, re-converts, or persons newly
> converted to our Holy Faith unless they are Negro
> or other slaves who have been born in the power
> of Christians who are our subjects and nationals
> and carry our express permission."

In the Islands the "wretch" Bishop Las Casas
(thank you, David Walker)
Accepts God's gift to the New World,
Proposing that each Spaniard will import Twelve
(that number again) Africans to this Eden,
For the prosperity of God and Country.
His. Theirs.

When there are no more Africans in Spain
They are supplied from Africa.
> They who conquer rule with a rod of iron.
> Our earthen pots are shattered to pieces.

This Eden proliferates in gold, tobacco, sugar.
Trees of Life and Knowledge
Fill the mouths of Europe with the luxury of evil,
Ours with sighs and ashes.

Christian Europe sends ships and fight among themselves
For the honor of saving us, We who Languish in Darkness.
For the *Asiento* and the profit of supplying Spain with slaves.
For the greater honor and glory, for the love of God.

ii. Nations rise against Spain, at last
Jealous of her success in spreading the Word.

French Francis frets,

> "The sun shines for me as for others.
> I should very much like to see the clause
> in Adam's will that excludes me from my share
> of the world. God did not create these lands
> for Spaniards only."

Sir William Cecil blasphemes, says the Pope
Has no right to divide the world
And not give any of it to England.
Elizabeth declares that the sea and the air are for all men.
Hakluyt says that with the assistance of God
(with a little help from Hawkins and Drake)
The Queen will increase her dominions,
Fill her banks, and (he uses the Word)
Reduce
Many pagans to the faith of Jesus.

Britannia grows fatter and whiter
On her diet of Black flesh,
Cements the stones of Liverpool with blood.

IV

i. It's the time of the Second Coming,
We feel his weight again.
Jesus sails the Middle Passage.
Sailing to Birmingham
Where Baptists bomb churches and children's bodies.
Sailing to Boston
Where Catholics bomb bussing and children's minds.
Sailing to Jonestown
Where a self-proclaimed Living God commands
His own slaves, "Bring the babies first"
To the sweetened poison of his power.

Jesus sweetly sounds his name in the believing ear
Of Captain John Newton

(later reverend and psalmist)
Who clutches his Bible to his expensively-suited breast,
Preaches two services each Sunday from the deck
To the legitimate majority in the noisome hold
Via TV sets provided by the Company.

Jesus walks the waters, leaves tracks of fire
To guide the shark-disciples—those perfect, silent
Witnesses that follow the ships, waiting
For men who prefer death
In their own dignity. In their own hours of
Decision they make their leaps of faith
Back into the pure, innocent savagery of
Nature's razor-tooth mouths.

ii. Jamestown,
We come to Jamestown.
In time our sweat and blood bloat
The lean vampire mistress there
Into the Great Whore of Memphis, Charleston,
Mobile, New Orleans, who wallows
In her beds of cotton, stuffing it between her legs
To make her ravaged abomination sweet
For the merchants of the earth.

> *Who are these coming to the sacrifice?*
> *To what green altar . . .*

Slaves of love and fear,
Slaves of naked devotion to another white god
Who betrays them again, in green Guyana,
Commands them to "die with dignity"
In a White Night orgy of murder and suicide.
How green
Africa was. How Black
Her maidenhead. How red the altars.
Jesus, how the ships come,
To JamesJonestown, JimCrowtown,

Jesustown, to "America for Jesus,"
Congregations for the Lord in the holds,
Vats of cyanide for the Last Supper.

In Virginia the Assembly legislates,
The churches cheer assent that
"Baptisme doth not alter the condition of a person
as to his bondage or freedom . . ."
Baptisme doth not alter.
Baptisme doth not alter . . .

A bishop in Africa languidly waves his hand,
Baptizes slaves going down to the sea in chains,
Knowing it does not alter.
        Nat Turner! Do you hear?
        Do you hear, Nat Turner!

V

i. The issue of the Harlot's womb
Fight among themselves.
Some believe it's to free Christian slaves,
But it's as much a merchant's war to depose the King
Who keeps the Whore's bed pure and white with Cotton.
Then they who were conquered among themselves
And ground into the earth in humiliation,
Wash their robes in blood, wear them
To hide their nakedness in the night,
Reclaiming their wasted land
In the burning sign of Constantine.

     See, see where Christ's blood streams in the firmament!

ii. The War ends. The wars go on, the Knights of the Cross
Ride Terror and Murder, a two-horse race,
Into the next century, out of the night,
Out of their sheets, into magazines,

TV interviews, public shootouts,
Perfunctory guest appearances in American courtrooms.
Miss Mary
(blonde, sweet, petite as jockeys must be)
Promises to fix the niggers'
Bacon by riding all the horses of the Apocalypse at once.
The symbol is the same It means the same.
Now the odor is familiar to Constantine.
He knows the stench.

iii. Now this is the only true miracle ever witnessed:
Black people also worship and love this God.
Who has let them drown
In His blood,
And in their own.

ONE OF MY OWN

I have a god
Not like yours
Right for me
Small for my pocket
A Yingyang god/dess
Olorun and Onile
Halved down the middle
Good to me when I'm good to you
And through my pocket pleasures me
With divinest fingers—
Immediate reward when memory fails
To curse you for the poisoned bread your children eat—
The hand of the other half is a razor,
And when I'm not good
My little god/dess gets me living in this life
And slices another nanometer
Through my dickstring.
What more would you
Need to make
You love?

SLOW DRIVERS

Smug
or timid
not always the old
behind the wheel
they sit right
in the middle of the Law
as if it belongs to them;
as if they will inherit
what's yours as well
with your life;
keep you behind them
on narrow roads
hours, days
it seems
all your life!
as if it belongs to them;
it's not that you're reckless
or foolish
or would have them
that way, equally dangerous;
but you must be getting on, getting on
not loitering behind them
where they bait
your fury
and impatience across double lines
into blind
curves
making you wait wait
wait
wait
wait
wait until you savor the heady salt
of risk on the palate
and pull out

seeing death
in their eyes
when they smirk at you
as you pass

Spirituals, Gospels

Nothing on earth can make me believe them.
I cringe before the weary forgiving
of that Lord whose blood whose blood drowned our gods,
who survived the slave pens
where, thrown in by the masters
as bait to control the chattel,
they nevertheless took Him, made Him blacker
almost than the masters could endure.
Yet still today, still they sing
to be washed white in His glory,
sing of a bitter earth, where my confusions deceive me
    with sweet seasons at my door,
    with dream or memory of savanna and plain
        where the lords are elephant and lion;
        jungle where the deaths of lesser gods
            feed back into its own resurrection;
        canopied rain forest, all that life in the trees
as the heaven I know.
And whales swim in our oceans.

Yet my own blood weakens, freezes
at their sound, the "unearthly harmonies"
alone probing the faith in my doubt,
making me fear the joy that for the duration of the music
crushes resistance utterly, utterly.
I know that's who I am, what I am
when the souls of Black folk sing.
While the Soul of Black folk sings.

From a Person Sitting in Darkness

Very deadly serious, the religious white Christian
lady on TV said God wanted this country
to bomb the Devil out of whatever Yellow Evil
disguises itself as old folk and children.

But the rain,
the rain in trees is a harmony of single drops
on single leaves.

It does not hear me,
the heathen, rage, or the godly rant
their rituals, taboos, formulas, chants
for gods of every conception.

Cancer cells hear nothing
in spite of prayers,
dividing between love and fear with
        admirable efficiency
into the gods that people heavens and hells,
killing grounds,
nirvanas for the just and wicked.

Divines and scholars debate
Creations
and Last Things, angels die,
dance on subatomic stages.

The swaddling giant GIGO[1]
spews out with terrible efficiency
another generation of divines, missionaries at the door,
TV evangels with fatuous smiles such as
who say, "The difference between this country

1. GIGO: "garbage in, garbage out." Garbled input to a computer produces a garbled
output.

and the Comma Nests
is we have God."

Thus the male of the species delivers himself
when "this country" was bombing the Devil
out of his lady's Yellow Peril, for God.
You might think that's what *he* was talking about,
but No, not them, nor the Red American Indians
nor the Black American Slaves
nor the Brown American Anybodies
who would've been glad to know that one day
there would be such a difference:
we have God.
But No, these Christian American serious whites
very deadly wanted to pray in school.
No. Wanted their children to pray.
No. Wanted my children
to pray to their deadly god in their language,
not knowing how dangerous it is
to erect towers to that peevish One
who shattered common speech into GIGO's babel,
scattered man over the face of the earth.

No (the trees). He is everywhere
betrayed by the commonness of his guises,
staked on the dunes between Arab and Jew,
whimpering and hiding in terror from Protestant
and Catholic bombs on the Emerald Isle.

No, the trees do not heed them,
nor spiders, worms, or cockroaches
locked in their eternal mortal dances
who will inherit what is left of the earth.

What is left of the earth,
counterpoint to the harmony of rain and trees,
the death of GIGO,
the Third Coming will be

in the heart of the atom
(you have been looking in the wrong direction).
All the qualities of the Sacred
are in the *Power* of the strong force,
so clean, so pure, it holds together
the mutual repulsion of its components
and what Church has ever done that?

The *Danger of the Sacred*
is Goddeath, at the heart of the nucleus
(ask the Japanese, ask the Japanese).

The *Mystery of the Sacred*
in the elusive quarks, Goddeath's angels,
the houri of Allah, minor deities of the Pantheon,
attributes of all gods,
Up, Down, Strangeness, Beauty, Charm,
and the Truths of all gods.

The *Secret of the Holy*
is hidden in the confinement of the quarks,
their enslavement to Goddeath
who will free them at man's peril
as the Japanese will testify.

The Square Deific of nature's forces
is nonsecterian, at least as reasonable
as other systems, the beauty of the unified field
at least as lovely as any other,
but never mean, hypocritical, murderous
(ask the West African what happened to his ancestors.
Ask the Native American what happened to his land.
Ask the Person Sitting in Darkness what happened to his light).

Why not? Well, why not? I'd like to ask them
to clarify one thing: Is that the only difference,
to have God? I think they were being modest.

ONE MORE WORD

The universe already thrashes
in a big fishnet of words
because everybody thinks nothing is
and nothing had without a name

so I named her a word
that hummed in the wetness of a bad night
because she was escapable
and undiscoverable

as the universe in a fishnet
and my hands were wet for her
but the naming was as good
as when God said

"Give them names Adam"
and Adam named
better than anyone ever
until I named her Lover

in a bad night blowing wetness
and the universe kicked at the net
in a storm
and the thunder said Never.

Another Creation

In Egyptian myth Atum-Re
masturbates into the primordial mud,
life begins, and there is another creation.
And why not? But just as my hunger and doubt

had almost become reconciled
I learn the joke that's the meaning of it all.
Now I see the gods, each solitary,
straddling the universe,

busy hands stroking myriads of suns and letting go,
speechless with the gift of laughter
that makes us like them,
because without the redundancy of creation

immortality is a lonely business.
Like them I'm tempted to laugh
if I find that what I have left
in my hands is a poem.

To Waste at Trees

Black men building a Nation,
My Brother said, have no leisure like them
No right to waste at trees
Inventing names for wrens and weeds.

But it's when you don't care about the world
That you begin owning and destroying it
Like them.

And how can you build
Especially a Nation
Without a soul?
He forgot that we've built one already—
In the cane, in the rice and cotton fields
And unlike them, came out humanly whole
Because our fathers, being African,
Saw the sun and moon as God's right and left eye,
Named Him Rain Maker and welcomed the blessings of his spit,
Found in the rocks his stony footprints,
Heard him traveling the sky on the wind
And speaking in the thunder
That would trumpet in the soul of the slave.

Forget this and let them make us deceive ourselves
That seasons have no meanings for us
And like them
We are slaves again.

Symbiosis

You have been tricked out of your element
by versemakers and songwriters; keep them
as hostages for their ignorance and let's exchange
means of survival.

I'll give you what I've used up,
or has used me, and you'll undress
the way trees do in that world better
without us.

Here, Poem, is hate. Here is evil,
and fear. I give them as freely,
as imperatively as you do the itch of summer's hot weeds
and the white fat things

you hide in leaves. Your cacophony
of birds is fair exchange
for the sorrow we feel at the loss of days,
however they go.

Your swarms of gnats dissolve in our tears,
we wink with your butterfly wings at our own cruelties,
our bellies growl when you rumble overhead,
and the thunder

with which you fill vacuums
is indistinguishable from our farts.
We try to deceive you with success
and you expose us,

scurrying on possum hands into our hollow hearts
and fastening your teeth there.
Ah, Poem, we should be true to each other
because an acorn will do

for what genuine faith there is.
Let's celebrate this truce then

for we have become what we are
in creating each other,

I more than ever when I didn't know
where we were going, or why.

Poems Like This.

When things start getting away
Those first bites of time
Come out of sensations
That once set the hooks in the brain—
The lines slackening,
Inevitably losing the taste of the bait:
See how deep down and far out
The mind has to go from the bank
To bring back real bubbles for the tongue,
The most stunning pain,
The authentic feel of penetration.
Forgive me:
Even under the lull of those yellow sheets,
Yellow light,
I knew the sharks would come
To feed in the pool that flooded your room
And even then I was thinking of the right words
For the small tactile things
That would nibble at my mind's version
Of the way things merely felt
From one feeling to the next.
Forgive me :
While you were away from me I was inside you
Trying to remember how deep,
How warm and slick, how cool.
It hasn't kept the sharks away.

Two Figures on Canvas

Here in this foreground of sunny Italian fields
She accepts exile as obligation to art.
This one, as all the others,
Has brought her here for his own need
From her harsher land beyond those background towers
Where even a stable and clean straw served
The kind of need they all understand.
He smiles in appreciation at his image of her.
And she, in spirit, must smile because she is aware
Of her renascence among women,
And is woman enough to smile.

She takes and comforts the child.
She assumes her pose from habit, endurance.
She accepts the gambit of heavy satin gown
In fashion with a wistful fancy
For the extravagant cascade of solemn Latin and feudal music:
But she laughs at his need for those moons,
For those pancake haloes.

Portraits

On the four-to-twelve shift
on the open door of a locker
a pinktipped kneeling nude
cups, lifts, and squeezes her
self in hands too small
for her own abundance of glossy goodness.
Her smile is warm, sincere.
She is perfectly innocent.
Scotchtaped below her
is a longhaired man with the saddest
blue eyes, too much a gentleman to look up,
but innocently ahead, his hands
pointing the eye to the exposed
dripping heart, red as Mars.
He is perfectly serious.
Who wouldn't be proud of a daughter like that?
What a blessing to have such a son.

RECITAL

For Don Adcock

Halfway back into our cups that night,
the party breaking up,
I heard him say to someone, "I love the sound
your ears make when they wiggle."
I would've known him better for that,
but in all these years we've moved
in different circles of unknowing,
seldom touching: his music, mine words.

When I heard him play last night I knew
the flute must be the right instrument for a man
with ears to hear things like that.
His covered by his hair,
I knew who I thought him to be,
but more human than that halfgod—
though less than we because he both heard and played
the music he made in us, and moved us in our private spheres
to make us more like him,
and the gods whose ruins we are—
whose music is the purest thing left in us.
It still haunts us sometimes from the woods
and still defies imitation; but because he hears
it and tries for us, he helps make us
the best we'll ever be.

LOVERS

They have been our mortal fools
Since we stood erect, cooked meat, made gods—
Perhaps winning our first laughter
With their windy breathing, their verses,
Their keepsakes, their plagues of anniversaries.
Even now, wave after wave of the air we breathe
Is broadcast with the babble of their ballads,
Making us unwitting celebrants
Of their discovery that robins sing,
The moon shines, violets grow, spring
Arrives, summer endures, and trees and seas
And breezes whisper, all for them. And all

Stop, fade, die, are mute, mocking, when love is gone,
Absent, late. Theirs is no ignoble or trivial pain
That, little less than death,
Has such wide capacity and power
To turn bitter, curse man, beast and stone;
Makes desolation of vast seconds that pinch the brain
To despair, suicide, murder. Yet sometimes in rare
Madness, or pure sanity more awesome,
One will force its shape and sound into an art
That chokes laughter when we recognize
The single human image of its transfigured wisdom.

GREENHOUSE

First a fable, and then the truth. We sensed
The execution of the plants at their stands
As they guarded us at door and frozen window
From the light's surprise entrance to the darkest room
We'd known—as if an evening star had collapsed
Into the house's basement room where we
Lay dazed in the singularity of a black
Hole in time; our bodies' gravity twisting
Space into the bed's depression, we cancelled
Natural laws, displaced all other matter
And light into an opposite system, beyond
Our control and caring. But when that light
Exploded past our plants faster than its
Own limit, we turned from each other's arms to the sounds
We imagined: ghosts of footsteps overhead,
And Venus's plant, the sundew, pitcher plant,
Cobra lily, sidesaddle flower and butter-
Wort shrieking warning silences and dying for us.

First the fable, and now a truth. But one
Is as strange, has as much charm, color, and beauty
As the other. What matters is the energy of
Its telling, else why do the heathen rage,
The godly rant? In truth, they are the same
If based on what we see (even through our
Instruments) and most of all, feel, or expect
One day to prove on the senses. It does matter
That matter is, and that what matter isn't
(Except energy and the unified field) is not.
This is truth: an elegy for whatever died
From neglect while we made love. That night "the music
Of the spheres" was organ music, and when the pipes
Burst, the poor devils froze to death in their places.
We were in the darkest room we'd ever
Known, a true house, a real room, and even

Though half buried in a hillside, was neither
A Swelling in the Ground, nor monarch Thought's
Dominion—not those abstractions. It was our darkest
Room because when I put the light out (an
Ordinary light) we had only each
Other, nothing but the comfort and solace
Of our bodies, bodies no denser than all
Ordinary matter and would rot in graves
Less intensely dark than that room where we
Could have stared openeyed forever, forever
Blind waiting for something to emerge,
Reveal itself, take shape. It was that absolute.
The desperate hunger of our bodies, the need
For simple touch, for light, for dark in which
To find the truth about our need—that's what
Devoured the light and left the moon hollow.
That's why the dark was real: we discovered
That deprivation in love is hunger, is pain
Too common, too necessary to sublimate in fables.
That was truth's light and dark: the necessity
Of pain in our world to make the joy of its
Complete reversal in each other's love with
Even the most primitive harmony that sets
Us apart from the ghostly lives upstairs:
The smooth surprise of tongues in our mouths; our hands
And backs shaping themselves to their own curves and
Hollows from their instant recall of absence.
And it was we and not the spider, coffee,
Coleus, philodendron, African violet,
English and devil's ivy who sang God God
I love you in that dark, because in none
Of the perfect days of unvarying gold had we
Seen as much. That was the truth. Now the fable again.

All My Live Ones

Penny accepted the Alabama neighbor's green meat,
Died in our swept-dirt back yard
Near the black wash pot, her brown spot penny-
Side up. My mother's dog, but like
All pets, with no sense of justice:
After forty years she still haunts
Me, innocent of her death, with
These images. My mother en-
Trusted to me the folly of love,
The daily care of caring for them,
And the rest were all mine to lose,
Mockery in their dying
And more than fear in running away.
Rex, ears clipped, tail bobbed, escaped
Into Pennsylvania nowhere
In a cloud of flea powder for no reason
That a twelve-year-old could know.
Mickey Midnight, the stray gift to me,
Sick in bed from school, black
As only cats can be, stuck it out
Only long enough for the perfect name
And took it with him.
Fulton (after Sheen, the bishop,
For his round skull cap), my one canary
Died so soon after he'd learned to sing,
Finally, that I wondered if song
Were worth the cost, And last: Sinbad.
One morning before Pharmaceutical Latin
In nineteen fifty-two I watched him die
My nearest death, between my absent brother's
Bed and mine, stretched out, rasping, so closely
Watched I knew and remember which half-second
Distemper tore his last breath out.

But the people: how different.
Since nineteen thirty-three

I've been the key to immortality:
All it takes is loving me:
Both parents, who had me
When they were young; the brother
Who left me there that morning
Alone when that dog died;
A wife who let me go
With her life, our three sons;
Another wife bringing
Her hostages to fortune,
Two daughters; all the lovers.
What will I do?
They are all here. At my age what will I do
With only a bird and a dog long ago?
I cried for days. For days and days.

"School Days"

Her surprise gift is a photograph,
A six-year-old with an absurdly large white bow
Atop severely combed-back hair.
"When I saw it, I thought it was my sister."
I look at them,
Astonished by the woman I know
Waiting in the child's eyes and mouth,
In whose repose I fight the lure of blood
Into forbidden vessels.
Yet she had not recognized herself
Coming back from the past
Had become her own sister.
But because she is here now
I am continually re-making myself,
The past no more immutable than one's identity.
     I hear the taped despair of old music
     below the current of familiar frequencies.
     Like arctic terns guided by infrasonic surf
     thousands of miles away, my memories
     make the long migrations between the poles
     of future and past. I take her back there
     to the boy, give him a glimmer of her
     waiting with all that love, filling in
     some of the empty spaces. Only music
     gives me the bridge to the chasm of self-pity
     I felt hearing Johnny Ace's "Saving My Love for You,"
     and "Never Let Me Go"; throttled to romantic
     delirium by the syrupy strings of Aquaviva's
     "Beyond the Next Hill"; never able to keep my hands
     from myself, but never in joy. In the collapse
     of present and future into my old discontent
     we change that,
     becoming our own and each other's parents,
     children.
From the picture to the woman, to the paradox.
If I had known, I may not have needed her.

If She Sang

I would feel better if it were song I heard:
in the kitchen, amid the harvest of utensil noise
she sows around her like dragon's teeth;
or in the corner of our room
where she stitches to herself, quietly
until she bursts into speech,
so far from both of us
that a third person is its only possible medium.

"What did you say?"
I sometimes challenge and retreat,
taking the risk of intrusion
because no alarm that brings someone who loves us
is false.

Yet I would feel better
if she sang.
I understand song and could enter
uninvited into its world;
but in her moments of self
and counterself is a dimension with room
for the two only, where even love
is suffered with the patience reserved for fools.

DARA

When they start pulling you out
The anesthesiologist tells me I may look.
I stand and look over the tent
That hides your mother's body from herself.
I look and see
The slick wet head, deceptively black,
That will dry to your nappy red.
Tugs at you. Cuts. Cuts.
I understand your fear, reluctance.
You had clung so tightly
Inside, attached so uncertainly to the womb
Against the tide of blood that threatened to sweep you away
Down the toilet where she sat, head bowed,
Watching the flood.
Bargaining for you (Yes, with that promise she keeps)
With the god she might as easily have cursed.
Except that it might be you who paid.
Cuts. Cuts. Your mother's flesh, muscle, fat, blood.
They tug and tug now
After you had held so tightly
In that micro-ocean, your gray eyes shut
In desperation, clinging to your only hope,
Yourself, imitating her position, her purpose,
Hugging and bowing into yourself,
Into your own stubborn strength,
Curving your feet so tightly against you
They would need casting,
The tide flowing, seeming to drain, leech you
Fair black child
You are free,
Out, I tell her, second daughter,
Dara. The Beautiful One, last
Child (before they close her)
Is free.

Liberation

It's one of those little mean
Coincidences our world turns on.
Only last night I read Sexton's
Celebration of her uterus,
And here I am this
Morning, sitting by
Without use in Helen's room
While the surgeons' hands work busily
Removing hers. And I celebrate
That sacred part of her
That has withstood, for mere human love,
The trials and crucifixions of her body.
Miscarriage and birth and
Miscarriage and birth and
Pain, and pain. I always said
"We" lost the baby, just as I said "we"
Have a daughter, but I could say nothing
About that pain. She lay there
In the middle of it, while I
Could only stumble
Around its
Edges,
Terrified of its
Vaguest touch. At the ends of our dark nights
Together, after her pain had shriveled
My little mortal soul to dust,
I could never decide which made the crueler joke:
God as male bungler
Or God as female masochist,
But the survivors were women,
She and the two lovelies
Who clung to that sacred part
For mere human love, and were delivered.

And I celebrate that woman
Who stood bleeding two years

On her magnificent pillars
Like another wonder,
Bleeding her human blood,
Baptizing me as I crawled under her
My belly lower than the ground.

And God, dam the blood of the lamb.
I celebrate the merely human bleeding womb
That brought salvation to us all.

GOD'S BUTTON

The god my child conceived last night
Can press a button on a machine, she said,
And make you grow, even when you're sleeping.
The reality of an idea, as god is,
Is no less than that of a starfish or pinebox;
Its power may be greater than an earthquake, volcano,
Or no less than absolute, eternal.
Her improvisation, then, must have caused
The drowsy inhabitants to jostle for room
To admit her Buttonpusher to the pantheon.

Then, "God is love," she said.
But the jury of my senses and I said No,
If he is who must be absolute, eternal;
Love is not both—is more real than its idea—
But only human; we remember the evidences
Of growing through catastrophes of gain and loss,
The "discontinuous phenomena" that shape life's cusps
And surfaces when no truth, honor, pride, duty,
Or any idea, could resist any given moment,
Or even memory, of animal penetration and affection
(the way Helen walked pigeon-toed through the snow
made my decision between her life and another's;
remembered round pressures, the small warmths of faces
pressed between neck and shoulder;
voices dying away, fading,
human only).
God is love if eternally, continuously human,
Longer than the moment it took him to fake death,
Perverting it into faith, doctrine: Idea.

Love has made me grow, though not so straight
As the pines I saw through her window,
Waking her this morning. In the early sun
They were themselves spears of light growing up

As our lives run down.
Whose finger is on which button?
As mine runs down I make progress
In knowing one thing God is not.
Death is eternal, absolute, animal, human.
God is love as long as one of us lives.

The Death of Another Fellow

1. It's April, the month I can't escape,
Thick with paradoxes, when
So many things have ended or begun.
I am pulling the lawn mower through the back door
When the sun blinks and freezes the space
Where my unwitting sinister eye sees the black shape
Vanishing between the two concrete blocks laid end to end
On the sloping earth beneath my window.

Now I unwillingly know the secret
Of his hiding place: he hadn't been far from home
When he'd left those shed skins
Along the rear wall of the house
Those years before. Not far at all.
And the warm driveway was his porch,
Where he'd surprised Helen
Once too often. It must be killed
Because of the girls, she told me.
How can she let them go out into the yard?

But until he became so careless
He never revealed where he lived.
And I swear: I thought I didn't know.

2. It's a simple, mindless chore, cutting grass.
You can easily lose yourself in meditation
Going back and forth across a yard
As I do this Sunday morning.
It's less easy if you're being constantly
Watched, back and forth,
As I am.

> *I know who you are, African forebear*
> *coming to give me corn and fertility;*
> *incarnation of our dead, unborn children;*
> *Indian ancestor, great grandsire, spear*

> *of the war gods, rain-bearer;*
> *and you, the more "civilized" of my burdens,*
> *tempting me with wisdom and guilt.*

I have little enough of one, none of the other.
Because I wasn't meant to be alone
I married twice, but continued to burn.
Now there are old lost loves to remember,
To wonder what became of,
For whom I might have been cutting this grass.
And sons, who might have been doing it for me.

The farther away from him I get
The further he comes up, black and straight,
From between the stones, outlined
Against the house, watching me
In a curious, friendly way.
In spite of the enmity
It's hard to resist that functional beauty,
The symmetry of its purpose in living.

> *I see you, old buddy. At this distance*
> *are you following only the sound of the mower*
> *back and forth, or is it me?*

You play with fire. And your children burn.
For the love I found wholly incarnated in Cathy's arms,
Eve's breasts, Kay's hair, Suzy's lips,
Annie's thighs my sons burned without their father.
Alas, alas that ever love was sin!
But that *was* love, the better part of wisdom.
Nevertheless, why keep the grass cut
And the yard fenced in
And free of snakes if there are no children?

> *But you are inside the fence*
> *and that's as far as I can go*
> *before I must come back to you.*
> *And still you rise from your hole*
> *the farther away I go,*
> *my fixed foot leaning after me*
> *but vanishing if I approach you.*

I need the distance more than you;
but there's this goddamned fence.
And here in the corner of the yard, the mowing
Is difficult where Helen had the garden plot
The year before the first baby was born.
The grass has overgrown it now, and surrounded
By the drainage ditch, and raised higher
Than the level of the yard, it resembles an island
Or burial mound.
She made things grow there in profusion.
Lettuce, beans. tomatoes, squash, eggplant, corn.
And the fruit in the woods beyond the fence:
She never went over there, afraid of the snakes.
And she wants the yard free, her home safe.
I tell her
        he is harmless, and replaces
            small, lesser, more numerous, flabby evils
(and maintains a balance in my nature)
She says: it is better to marry than to burn,
But I was not meant to burn with you.
Nor will I let my children.

3. I leave the mower running out of his
sight, behind the redwood fence that extends
twelve feet from the wall of the house into the yard.
I go into the basement for the B.B. gun,
a rake and spade, out the front door
around the side of the house, behind him.
At the corner of the house I peer
around, brace myself against the
house, and sight the gun on the opening
between the two blocks. His head emerges, waving
toward the sound of the still running
mower. I aim at the back of the
small head and try to stop wavering. I
miss the first shot and he
vanishes. I cock the gun, feeling cowardly, and
foolish, hoping no neighbors see me.

He emerges again and I steady
myself. Another
miss? So. I've got to face him.
I go through the gate, carrying my
rake and long-handled spade. I pull over one of the
concrete slabs with the rake, and then the
other, and in the hollow space underneath

> *from the mass of black coils*
> *the head comes up and the spade goes*
> chuk chuk chuk *(Stop!)* chuk chuk *through the body*
> *into the cool clayey earth.*
> *The sun is blinking, freezing the images*
> *of his movements. His lidless, unblinking eyes*
> *mock and accuse me in cold intelligence,*
> *its sacrifice transforming it into Serpent.*
> *The head falls back among the coils and guts,*
> *the mouth opening and closing in gasps.*
> *as if to localize the pains.*
> A small movement. A nest? Young ones? A family?
> No. Serpents are solitary, live alone.
> That is its tail.

I cover him with dirt,
Bury it there under my window and replace the stones.
It was so helpless after all,
So easy to kill.
And my own fears.

4. Now it's June. Walking up the front steps
With my oldest daughter, I hear rustling
In the dry leaves at the side of the porch.
I look over the wrought iron rail
And see a black snake, smaller than the one
I killed, moving along the front wall. Above it,
On a bush, a mockingbird is chirping at it
In agitation, feathers ruffled, wings outspread.
I take my child into the
House, tell her to stay there while I
Kill a snake. I get the spade from the basement

And go back out to the front yard.
It has gone. So has the bird.
I go around the house and find nothing.
Back inside, Shani asks if I killed it.
No. It was gone.
But Daddy, it was harmless anyway and wasn't
Going to hurt anybody.
I look at her, unbelieving. No, I said,
It wasn't going to hurt anybody.

*Then what was it I killed, what is buried
in the back yard under my window?*

IV

From *Leaning Against the Sun* (1992)

Eagle. Tiger. Whale.

I'm old enough to stand,
a boy looking at himself
in the long mirror of a chifforobe,
Black child with sandy hair
tightly curled, hazel eyes.
I haven't learned the words,
I photograph everything into my cells:
my little yellow dress with puffed pleated shoulders
and my little pearl buttons;
my little high-topped white shoes and yellow socks;
my little blue ribbon somewhere.
The room behind me is dark,
nothing in the mirror but me
as in a spotlight, yet I feel her presence,
my 17-year-old mother, beautiful,
leaning somewhere behind me.
      No one can explain what I've seen, a slim Black woman lying
on her back, red geyser pumping from her open mouth, she stares into
the ceiling's yellow eye. I see her from her right, the foot of the brass
bed, my head three feet high. Someone screams "Lord God Lord God
he done shot the woman" while the soft splash, splash. I stand so calm,
seeing, until somebody yells "Git that chile outta here." Who knows
who knows how I got there from next door, visiting Aunt Annie over
in Gadsden, for neither mother nor father is there to tell me "Forget it."
                                          don't tell don't
tell James Albert's sister whispers in the dim coal shed.
She has hair everywhere,
the only subject, verb, object, adverb
I can put together.
It's my birthday, I come to her yard
to pick figs from their tree. James Albert's
daddy said I can, I pull a fig,
she whispers "don't tell, don't tell,"
I feel my hand disappear into the hot full-noon mouth
of Alabama's summer solstice,

lips, lips, tongue curling around, probing
the fruit from my paralyzed fist.
She changes my hands from left to right,
leaves me partially ambidextrous and stuttering
to describe it.
        Now that I've read a lot,
I've learned boxes of "reflection," "homicide," "initiation"
to put visions into,
just as we have done with *eagle tiger whale god*
with handles and edges to finger,
perfect and seamless,
not trying to break in, not letting anything out.
But there is that boy who can still do this:
In the Zaire rain forest a snow leopard like a ghost leaps
and with its perfect knives
slices open this box I've made.

Not Often near Such Water

I always swim parallel to shore,
No farther out than where I lose the bottom.
My family watches me, admiring, envious, uneasy.
My island-born wife who never learned to swim,
Our two daughters who are fish in the pool in Raleigh,
Here are unable to get past the first breaker.
Surf City it is. As early as the third day
We hear about and decide on the Outer Banks
Next time.
          I buy a Styrofoam surf board
Because I thought Dara had broken the one
That belonged to the kids in the next beach house.
She hadn't. The mother refuses our offer to replace it.
I take Shani and the board out to where I can stand
And try to help her ride
One wave in. She does her best,
But soon will have no more of the Atlantic.
          We play Monopoly, collect shells, the girls afraid of crabs.
When we walk the beach on a dark, windy evening,
I am on point, scanning the sand before us
For anything that scuttles.
I like the way waves slant in to the beach
In high wind and storm.
Someone is flying kites
Strung above the water
A long line of black sea birds.
A Marine chopper from Lejeune flies along the shore,
Its heavy growl drowning the surf's frothy rumble.
I daydream Hollywood's World War II LSTs
Hovering out there on the waves.
From the screened porch we watch mast lights, early morning boats
Belling through the mist, nets dipping side to side
For the flounder, snapper, blues and king mackerel
That we drive to the piers in the afternoons to buy.
          If only one of us swims,

He ought to make a show of benefiting from it.
Twice a day I swim and sun,
Enhancing my indifferent tan
Of African, Indian and Dutch ancestry.
I lie on the five-foot, coffin-shaped board
And paddle out to ride back in
The way I've seen the big kids do—
Out toward the inconceivable.
I crossed the Pacific in 1955
On the *USNS Sultan* to Clark Air Force Base.
Sea sickness is worse than death.
For two days I was worse than dead.
Then I'm given my shipboard duty for the week:
To go into a little room stacked with records
And play the likes of Les Brown, Ray Anthony,
The DeMarco Sisters, The Four Freshmen
Over the military Muzak system.
Out of hundreds of troops peeling potatoes,
Scrubbing pots, associating with food, God chose me away from it.
I had time for the deck, time to be blinded
By what the water does to the sun,
What the water does to the moon
Makes Turner seascapes come to life.
We steam past Bataan, Corregidor,
Shrouded in history on the port and starboard horizons.
Into Manila Bay, ships caught and sunk
Still show rusted hulls above the water.
I'd seen war movies enough for self-conscious patriotism,
The curious reverence one feels before memorials of death.
              Water particles don't move along a wave.
They move in circles as the wave passes by.
I'm a landlocked foreign body propelling myself
Against the disturbance that causes the wave phenomenon.
I've been carried away so quietly,
Up and down the swells so easily.
I look back and see far back
Wife and daughters and beach friends
Standing together, a little gathering

Looking out my way.
I hear almost no sound.
Quietly, quietly I will myself to match the ocean's ease,
abandon the surf board. To swim back to that small crowd.
The ocean seems to be holding its breath too,
Deciding.
I see that I'm not afraid.
The day FDR died they played the "Meditation" from *Thais*
All day on the radio.
I was twelve. I'd already begun violin lessons.
I'm frozen in an attitude between the (I'll make up a name)
Elm tree in the front yard
And cobblestoned Stranahan Street in Pittsburgh.
I've remained in that spot for forty years,
As though that's where I was the moment they announced his death
And began playing his favorite piece all day.
I've learned it, practiced, memorized,
Play it on Youth Day in Warren Methodist Church
When I'm (I'll make this up) about fifteen.
Each time I played it, hear it, I remember him.
There is nothing but fear itself.
            Can they see me?
If they knew how *calm* I am!
I'm out here in the first place and swimming so quietly back
Because I thought I was going to drown
In the pool on Washington Boulevard.
Some dissembling boys got me to jump in the deep.
I was ten or eleven and not long up from inland Alabama,
Had never been near such water. They pulled me out,
Laughing like bad boys, but not before I had memorized drowning.
I went to the other end and started learning to swim.
That was damned smart for a kid, instinctively right.

It's Joan, Shani, and Dara I'm swimming for.
Where was it, before the ships came?
Sierra Leone, Ghana, a dozen places,
Like Kunta Kinte or Gustavas Vassa
Taken from the forest and village to the coast.

But I was older, with two wives and five children.

Oh, the ships. The ships. We are dying, dying there still.

The sea is a choice.

I swim past the sharks to the children.

I'm too old for them to lose their father.

Uneasy, admiring, they see how calm I am, how far I've come.

This time, we will all go deeper into the forest.

DOMESTIC TRANQUILITY

I need a ritual to perform,
clean and sane, for this perfect washday,
the sun burning the top of my head
and forearms raised to the line,
the surrogate wind breathing
my wife's blouses, my daughters' dresses and jeans.
I need a formula to recite
free of mumbo jumbo and cant,
fit for me and this day, and I say
to hell with Kenmore, Whirlpool, Maytag,
who needs Norge, Wards, Westinghouse, GE?

When I strung my clothesline from the post
where the rosebush fans over the redwood fence,
I was careful not to scare the rabbit away,
come to the yard for clover,
crouching on the cool ground along the fence
among the mint that's grown high as my knees.
It sits in there still and breathless with revelation,
the laundry like sweet apparitions flapping overhead,
my presence humming through the intoxicating leaves.
I wish that kind of myth to give my daughters,
as free of cruelty and lies
as the vision of this small waiting animal.
Today I have only this day so perfect for the wash
drying by sun and wind, and a miracle for the rabbit
at peace under the rose bush.

Whose Children Are These?

1

Whose children are *these?*
Who do these children belong to?
With no power to watch over,
He looks at them, sleeping,
Exhaustion overwhelming hunger,
Barely protected with burlap from the cold
Cabin. Fear and rage make him tremble
For them; for himself, shame that he can do no more
Than die for them,
For no certain purpose. He heard about the woman,
Margaret Garner, in spite of the white folks' silence.
How she killed two of hers
To keep them from being taken back.
Killed herself after the others were taken back
Anyway. So she saved
Two. He couldn't save his Ellen and Henry.
Who do these belong to?
He doesn't dare kiss them
Now, but stands dreaming,
Willing these five back
To a place or forward to a time
He can't remember or imagine.
All he can do is find the place
He knows about. Leave now
Before dawn sets the white fields raging
And murders the North Star.

2

Grandsire, I kissed, blessed, chewed, and swallowed your rage
when I stood over the five you sent, warm in their beds,
and force-fed my stunned dumb soul to believe someone

owned, someone bought, someone sold at will
our children, Grandsire, I held them, I held them
as you could not, and revered that fierce mother
whose courage and whose solution I could not.
But we have not rescued them altogether.
We moved them through one dimension, from one killing
field to another on history's flat page,
1850s' slavery to 1980s' racism and murder.
Baraka has told us "They have made
this star unsafe, and this age, primitive,"
and it is so. I stood over each child sleeping
and looked at each child and wanted to know
who decides to break our hearts one by one by one.
The Greeks named it Tyche and made a goddess of chance.
Here they call it this god's "mysterious Will."
I have the children, but we have not saved them
from this primitive star, and I can't forgive.

10 September 1985

SPECIAL BUS

There's a bus, children with slack faces
in the next lane, on a field trip,
A sight to make a parent weep.
My culture and learning spreadeagle me
between what I feel and what I think I know,
force me to wonder why I've been five times
blessed or missed by Chance
and others not:
Dennis, Jerry, Josh, Shani, Dara—
twenty-three years from birth to birth,
risk increasing with each—
I'm about to beg the light to change,
or give in to what I don't believe I know.
A child turns and looks at me
with a light that can't be there
Please don't thank God
or my mom and dad will be forced to blaspheme
for my life.
The light changes.
The light dies.

STRANGERS LIKE US:
PITTSBURGH, RALEIGH, 1945–1985

The sounds our parents heard echoing over
housetops while listening to evening radios
were the uninterrupted cries running and cycling
we sent through the streets and yards, where spring summer
fall we were entrusted to the night, boys
and girls together, to send us home for bath
and bed after the dark had drifted down and eased
contests between pitcher and batter, hider and seeker.

Our own children live imprisoned in light.
They are cycloned into our yards and hearts,
whose gates flutter shut on unfamiliar smiles.
At the rumor of a moon, we call them in
before the monsters who hunt, who hurt, who haunt
us, rise up from our own dim streets.

Haunted House

1

The smallest bones in Helen's body
Don't dampen amplitudes as they should,
And, deep inside, her ears hurt. Her drums
Are set at such exquisite tension against my music
That a few measures from a sonata
Or a lyric I thought I'd forgot
Invites someone I loved or wanted
Forty years ago to take me back, away,
While she is distracted by threshold pain,
And makes the house tremble with her complaint
Against the noise,
However quietly my deference plays for her.

2

I've memorized dozens of songs, old
Now, and must be the last man alive
Who remembers the Four Tunes
And Savannah Churchill, and knows the lyrics
To "Is It Too Late?" and "I Understand,"
At 13 the first record I bought.
I thought my voice was good enough,
But girls wondered "Who is this strange
Boy singing to me?" They were charmed
But found it uncomfortable
And too odd to risk.
I married the first woman who didn't think so,
Who steered me arm in arm
Singing down dark streets
"The Nearness of You," who tried with me
My weird pastime of reading through
Verdi and Ellington scores.

Divorced and died away from that music,
I brought my life away on reels of taped 78s.

3

I sing to no one in this house,
Except alone, except to ghosts.
At the piano or stereo I cram
Eighth notes into my mouth with both
Hands, delight in the bite of their comet
Tails; sprinkle black pepper Thirty-
Seconds on my grits, crunchy crouton
Sixteenths on salads, make perfect Martinis
With black olive Quarter notes;
The powerful head-clearing Half note mints
Like the days of creation, prepare me
For the Whole, the cosmic egg,
The singular state of Nommo,
And I don't know that I'm not seeing
Blue Whales swim among the Pleiades when Rachmaninoff
And Ray Charles are transformed to pressure waves
In the liquid Tympani of my inner ear;
When Callas sings, Segovia plays, or Divine Sarah
Divines, I can't swear that I don't hear
The fifty thousand hair cells
Rippling in my organs of Corti as I follow
The electric impulses
Along the thirty thousand fibers of my auditory nerve,
And the brain quadrupling that in numbers of stars
That light folk to goon on galactic pilgrimages
To empty tombs, stones newly rolled away.
And everywhere throughout Andromeda
Young men in castle windows weep
For our loss, for Helen's noise, for Helen's pain.

Yardwork

1

These leaves blow here from others' trees: it's spite
That makes me not rake them till spring. This year
I choose Good Saturday as my first day
In the yard, and find under mine the reason
My neighbors don't let their leaves
Lie all winter. I was straddling the pile,
Pulling toward me, when I heard the squeak.
I who had to ask my neighbor the names
Of crepe myrtle and ligustrum, don't know this
Gunmetal blue creature crawling a bewildered circle
At my feet. A little white mixed in, round ears,
My mind insists "rabbit" to stop the reflex
Whose ignorance doesn't know a vole from a rat.
There are rabbits about, who eat the clover
When I don't cut grass often as Helen likes.
And last year I was forced to surrender to the one
I called Br'er, or Sis, the row of broccoli
And collards I tried to grow at the back door.
Even so, I hope it's not one of their chillun
I've raked or stepped on.
                                        It's going
In circles, I think, because it's hurt. It drags
A leg. There's blood on its hindquarters. I don't
Bend down to diagnose, I stand straight
As the rake I hold. Oh God there's a hole in the ground
Packed with fur, moiling with blue motion. The creature
Takes on stature as a mother, or largest
In a litter. And I'm not any kind of healer.
As a child
The saintly John Woolman saw
A robin sitting in her nest. As he came
Near, she went off, but flew

146

About "with many cries," concerned
For her young. The boy threw stones
And killed her. Pleased at first, then seized
With horror, he climbed the tree and killed
The birds, supposing that better
Than leaving them to pine away
And die miserably. Tender mercies.
　　At ten-thirty on a breezy morning the sun
Is mild, but there are no leaves now to filter
This light. I see those dark motions and comfort
Myself with a pathetic fallacy:
The one thing I can do is save them from
The cruel sun.
　　　　　　Except for a careful mound
Near the fence, my putting back, the yard is cut
And raked. And under that mix of sycamore and fur,
Life goes on as it will.

2

　　　　　　My daughters stand
On the bank and watch me free the creek. The water
Is usually clear, but people on Cooper Road
Use the street drain for whatever they choose: beer cans,
Broken toys, plastic and paper, old oil
That killed most of the crayfish that filled the stream
When it ran full from Taylor's Pond. Boys swam there
In spite of all he could say or do.
Who could blame him for breaking the dam? His drain
Pipe gave our back lots the diversions
Of running water. I built my own small dam
To amplify the sound, and watched the crayfish
Swim, clean, cleanly.
　　　　　　The girls want to see
What's under the leaves. Like me, they would prefer
Rabbits to mice. But I want nothing disturbed.

147

I've never seen that shade of living blue.
If that was the mother circling in the sun—
Well, Woolman didn't say how he did it.
I have gasoline. To pour and stifle. Or to burn.

I've raked a turtle shell heavy with mud
Onto my side of the creek. I can't tell the girls
If it's alive, but they lean over to watch
A lone, "dungy" crayfish struggle out of
The cloud I've stirred up. I roll the shell,
Alive or dead, back into the slow stream.

It won't be there tomorrow.
                                        Tomorrow the eggs
I hide for my daughters in the yard
Will be large plastic pantyhose
Containers, filled with foil-wrapped
Chocolates. Nothing to do with bunnies,
No "real" eggs that raise the dead.
Under the russet leaves, life
Will go on as it will. Or it will not.

What More?

My lawnmower has awakened the resident god of my yard
who rubs its leafy hand in anticipation
of troubling me again with one of its cruel koans,

this one a small bird dropped
from the sky, or thrown out,
out of the sweetgum tree

where I was cutting
that long triangle of grass outside
the back fence: put there

when I wasn't looking, it lies
on its back twitching half in and out of the swath
I cut a minute before.

I'm being tampered with again,
like an electron whose orbit and momentum
are displaced by the scientist's measurement

and observation. If I'd found something already stiff
and cold on the ground
I'd have kicked or nudged it out of my path:

but the just-dead, the thing still warm,
just taken its last breath, made its last
movement, has its own kind of horror.

I leave the small patch of uncut grass around it.
Back inside my enclosed yard
I see a brown thrasher come and stand over the body,

with some kind of food in its bill.
(I was careful to say "bill" and not "mouth.")
By the next time I cut myself around the yard,

I see the thrasher sitting on the fence above the still dead,
still holding whatever it has in its bill. I've described
it all accurately. What more could anyone expect of me?

Two Poems for Miller Williams

1. *Plot*

I'm not certain
                              yet
I don't believe I'll attend
her grave or stone
because there will be nothing here to see.
These flowers are for the living,
but not for me; I'd have bluejays screaming for her.
I was always birdboy, and she is flowergirl.
No. I'll stay at home
and cry in our bed alone
where I can remember
                              even now
we are dying of loneliness
in each other's arms.

2. *Theology*

Driving five-year-old Dara to school December 15,
she tells me that God was visible
when he created the world,
but that made him tired,
so he died, and went to heaven,
then he became invisible.

Suddenly I understand Lao-Tzu, Plato,
Augustine and Aquinas,
Barth, Tillich,
all those guys—

the whole thing.

Epigraphs

1

Melville B. Cox
—1799–1833—
Minister of Edenton St.
Methodist Church, 1831.
First American Methodist
Missionary to Africa, 1833.
"Let a thousand fall before
Africa be given up."
—Historical marker, Raleigh, N.C.

The man and his dates obsess me. Each day
I go to work or take my daughter to school
And pass his memorial I curse and swear,
Shake my head, or smile knowingly. This is all
I want to know about him, though he seduces
Me with motives, taxes my imagination
With scenarios of his death. Whose Africa
To give up, or keep for whose benefit?
Thousands fell to temptation, shook African
Trees, and black fruit fell into their salvation
Sacks, into the holds of their ships. Think of it:
An American missionary of that Peculiar
Institution in that place! With some
Humility he might have been British,
Who abolish slavery in their Empire

That year: Johannes Brahms and Alfred Nobel
Are born, Edmund Keane dies, Santa Anna
Is President of Mexico, Oberlin
College is established, Tennyson begins
In Memoriam, the American Anti-
Slavery Society is founded, Melville B. Cox
Dies in Africa. I hear him howling with bloody

Flux, see his innocent arrogance enrage
The gods there who drive him mad, or become a Host
For his intended converts. I don't need "facts"
To affirm the truth of this dark allegory.
He would've been better advised to stay home,
Read the papers and notices for slave
Sales, observe and preach to his neighbors, and devote
His nights and days to theodicy.

2

Much Madness is divinest Sense—
To a discerning Eye—
            —Emily Dickinson

I envy you, Mr. Blake,
set screaming at four
when God looked in through your window,
and never a moment's doubt.
I believe in belief
that drives one mad,
when the darkroom door
swings open onto a nova that burns all the images
to blank white   freeze dried naked   and you hear
the uniform hiss of background noise in space
roaring in your mouth—profound terror
after the fact
and not the prudent wager,
not ashamed to say
Yes that looks like God out there to me
yes there are angels in that tree
yes I see the ghost of that flea.
If you are mad, Mr. Blake,
it's not the poet in you: the sanest of men:
what God sends poets with rifles and missions
to the tops of towers, to shopping centers, holy wars?
What poets go?

153

Heaven isn't that far away.
    At fifty-four I can still scream, Mr. Blake,
though I've already seen in the eye of a Humpback whale
the doomed tolerance of your face at the window.
But I'm nearly as willing to let my mind go a little,
to lean against the sun,
for one more poem.

3

> The vices of mankind are active and able ministers of
> depopulation. They are the precursors in the great army of
> destruction; and often finish the dreadful work themselves.
> —Thomas Malthus, *An Essay on the Principle of Population*

Earth is not supporting us, we are dying
Of malnutrition, starving by millions,
Not doing enough to check populations.
We are failing as Protestants and Catholics, Jews,
Sunni and Shiite Muslims, Hindus and Sikhs.
We need more and more Faith, more Religions.
Or soccer would suffice, with daily world
Wide championships in Brazil and Brussels.

For the survivors, let them thank the god
Who wins that animals have no known worship,
Or sports, and there will be food enough for man
At last, for the worst that some animals do
(who kill their kind only to eat)
Is to kill their food by eating it.

4

This was not the work of God—it was the work of Satan.
      —A mother who survived a tornado in Albion,
         Pennsylvania, June 1985. Eighty-six dead.

But he once was Lucifer, outwitted from that proximate height,
From one abstraction to a lesser, stripped
And streaming gorgeous photons of morning light
Like an electron descending levels of energy
And belief to rest in the mind's underkingdom
Until aroused by her despair: she shifts him
From one hemisphere to the other, reassigning
Power, endowing him with God's jealous sovereignty
To make the horror bearable.
                            And who
Is he to question her theology of grief?
And how will she sleep nights now that she
Has transformed her enemy's will into *tornado,*
Reshaping with its twisted foot her wild
Heart into an altar's sacrifice for her child?

5

I knew God meant for me to win this one of these days.
He didn't let me down.
      —Reba McEntire, upon being voted Female Vocalist of
      the Year at the Country Music Association Awards, 1985

Now we lay us down to dream,
Things are better than they seem,
And every dog will have its day.
Pray and wait just long enough,
Being faithful, hanging tough,
He'll serve us what we order, "all the way."

Bumper signs say "PRAYER WORKS."
Some who pray are clearly jerks,

155

Who force Him to trivialize that terrible power.
Not even taking His name in vain,
Coaches pray to win the game,
And expect results within the hour.

Take Him now, for all He's worth,
Taking is our right by birth,
Adam won it with his fall.
Now we lay us down to dream,
Keep it little, keep it mean;
We've made Him in our image, after all.

SPORTSFAN

Its appearance is human.
And so it may be.

Certainly it exhibits humanlike feelings
in its doglike devotion and loyalty
to the jockspecies on which it exists in symbiosis.
Its lifecycle is seasonal,
during which and according to the fortunes
of its team it becomes dangerous—
murderous, suicidal, destructive of property
private and public.
Its herd instinct is deceptively passive,
displaying aggressive group behavior
at those sportingevents that sustain it,
give it identity and sense of self
and where its actions
and forms of communication
are embarrassing to human parents
and unsuitable for small children.
Its sexual activity
is also seasonally influenced,
interest and energy dissipated
or drained off through TV tubes.
Exceptions may occur
during Homecoming and Championship rituals
when it has been known to engage in genital display
and public copulation.

However, only a bigot
would insist that all
are ugly and loud,
barbaric and boorish
because of the majority.
They may be
some of your best friends

who never act in any way
that arouses suspicion.
It depends on the season.

But it is perfectly understandable
that you would not want
your daughter,
or your son,
to marry one.

WAR FILM: DYING FOREVER

In my living room 44 years later
the marine is running and wading
off the landing barge into the water,
onto the beach at Tarawa.

It must've been blue, it must've been loud,
Hellcats and Corsairs from the carrier going in,
mortar, small arms, battleships firing into the island,
machine guns chattering its name.

The tall strange trees ahead must've surprised him
for a moment,
it could've been beautiful, the surf,
all that sun and those trees, the feathery tops,
if the word exotic was known
to a steelworker from Pennsylvania,
if there was time enough,
running toward the sand
on *The Twentieth Century* with Walter Cronkite.
It's all black and white to me
from the photographer's perspective
who must've been one of the first on the beach,
then turned his back to the land
to film what was coming in from the sea.

And there, there is the exact moment, without firing a shot,
our Marine Harry Allmon from Homestead is hit by a round or more
from the Japanese soldier neither he nor I
will ever see,
and the moment he falls forward, pack, rifle, helmet,
the moment he stumbles in the water off Tarawa 1943
he is dead.

In war films on either side
I've seen the already dead,

like 20th century bodies,
stacked cordwood,
or rolling in surf, dead already forever.
But in this moving picture
this fall of this single man
traps me in his surprised sorrow.

Like the savior he would be
of ourselves
from all battles
who dies on demand for instant replay,
the technologies of war and film
keep him dying forever,
forever.

UNIFORMS

Again we say, of the North as of the South, that life
for us is daily warfare and that we live hard, like
soldiers.... The color of our skins constitutes our
uniforms...

—Richard Wright, *12 Million Black Voices* (1941)

They have never died in our uniforms
as we have in theirs.
It was easier to die in battle,
in the uniform of United States Colored Troops,
than on the plantations,
easier even at Fort Wagner, or Fort Pillow
when the gray demons shot and burned us
in our blue, prisoners of war.
We didn't want to die, but did.
All we ever wanted was to be free.
We died for that freedom, and theirs, too,
at Verdun, in the Argonne Forest,
and came back to familiar Chicago, Knoxville, Omaha
where they lynched us in khaki,
dishonored their own uniforms,
made a nightmare of their dream.
We didn't want to die at the Bulge,
at the Rhine and Arno Rivers,
on Pork Chop Hill, at Danang and Hue,
but we did,
becoming less sure whose freedom we were dying for.
For still, in places with familiar names
hooded men shame their faith as Christian Knights
of burning crosses,
enhance with sheets the color of the faces
that we often would die not to see, for just one day.

He didn't want to die in Memphis,
not because of a dream

not even for a dream,
but he did, in uniform,
in daily warfare,
and free, free of hate, because all he ever wanted
was that they could be as free as we are.

For Martin Luther King, Jr.
18 January 1986

ADAGIO

That morning you found your lights on,
battery dead, came back to the apartment,
walked in wet and blinking rain at me,
and we went back to the narrow bed

where always I hear the short *Ah!*
when I enter you.
Twenty years, I'll never see you again.
Barber's *Adagio* came six years later.

It's what we wanted for those three months,
for the days I'm going to live with,
like the strings sinking, and sinking.

Each time you come back I think
it will be the last time
and I won't know it,
like the last breath I don't remember taking.

Cello Poem

> I hear the violoncello, ('tis the young man's heart's
> complaint)
>
> —Walt Whitman

1

Another guest room on the poetry circuit   dim and elegant   dark furni-
ture   I drive the Hertzcar   looping and crisscrossing the state alone as
salvation from deadly smalltalk   Gambier   Wooster   Oxford   New
Concord   Athens   eight campuses in six days   I follow maps and direc-
tions sent ahead in strange hands

"Denise Levertov stayed here last year"   Well   What to say to that
    "How did she like it?"?   "Did she sleep well?"?   "Were her dreams
blessed or troubled by the presences of exhausted poets before her?"?

Yesterday a woman whom I will always love drove   twenty-seven miles
to hear me read her poem   Afterwards we delayed outside at her car in
an operatic November night so mild and unbearable I felt relief that our
past would remain where we'd left it   She drove away ten years further
back than she'd come   Alone in the heavy room six years away from
hometown neighbor   Pittsburgh and unreachable from Raleigh   I re-
member Cincinnati's WLW and American Airlines' *Music in the
Night*   lights off hours after midnight except for the glow when radios
had tubes and were warm and hummed at my bedside   I turn and find
it   Everything turns   I hear the violoncello

I couldn't have heard it before   never   I couldn't have
ever heard it in all the ugly duckling years when music
loved me only   When I became violin   piano   guitar
harmonica   When I chose as my favorite siblings
oboe   French and English horns   When the trained
sopranos   mezzos   tenors constricted my heart with
electricity and omnipotence   When I could have passed
out in the Westinghouse High School orchestra   for

164

joy   because I was in it   third chair   first violin   Even then
when   the physical beauty of the thing had sung to
my eyes   I hadn't heard it   Fascinated I'd see around
my music stand the girls holding the cello between their
wide-skirted legs   Its sound in their hands was
nasal   whining   but my dumb soul was dazzled by its
posture enshrined where it was

My first mature love at eighteen with the longest legs
I'd ever seen   called a boy's name   had played cello in
school before we met   I never heard her   but could
always see her doing it   When those legs were
mine they were the least of what we both wanted   not
for want of trying   Smart college kids   we knew what
we were supposed to know and kissed and kissed it all
without experience   our bodies denied us full use   shut
against us   We kissed away the difficulty we declared
marriage would give us time to solve: kissed standing
and lying   bodies grinding with such ferocity I'd ride
midnight streetcars home still engorged   groin aching
from her sharp pubic arch   a miracle we didn't become
nearly virgin parents on those winter evenings she
slouched to the edge of the chair before me   her wide
skirt at ease to be kissed   her endless legs molding me
into the shape of her cello

The bed gleams maple like her cello body in the dim room
sounding me   I hear Dvorak's concerto   in the allegro the
cello's sixteenth notes rippling under the flute and oboe
melody in and through me in 25 measures   and gone
before I can recover
            before I can recover I hear
                the cello's revelation:
                    its rich androgynous sound
is the voice of single trees
not Wagner's conventional horns for massed forest
or the string tremolos and slow trills for leaves and wind
                before I can recover I'm deafened

165

by the secret   trees of the virgin rain forests
celloing in the earth's holy lands
around the green belt of Zaire   Brazil   Gabon   Indonesia
before I can recover I hear a choir of cellos
war cry cello of the Zulu warrior
        kidnapped cry of the Yoruba father
                Comanche cello whose bow and strings
                    sing brief victory
dirty blues cello of a good woman done wrong
young French Chinese virtuoso cellist of Bach and jazz
dozens of women cellists who overcame mothers' doubts
of its unladylike demands   lovely   like woman and horse
aesthetic   sensual in their affinities
Spanish and Russian cellos of the old interpreters
                    Kali cello of the slipping strings
                Charli's cello   first mature love
        between whose knees I wove a timespace mobius
to keep me each moment
where I would be
in this room alone:
                    I see it all:
            she played the cello   she loved me
        I left that music back with her   but around the mobius
strip again we reverse positions   cello between my knees
playing
like the old men Casals   Rostropovich   Starker   This time
I choose interpretation and wisdom over virtuosity
        Alone I have no one to tell what I hear and see
            how stunned I am with its fullness
                my only despair that
I have no one to tell   not Helen at home whose ears hurt
to the noise she hears   I'd had to let go the siblings
whom music   who loved me   sent as lovers.
Before I can recover, it is morning.

2

Through the window at the kitchen sink,
I see white dogwood blaze across the grass.
I wash morning dishes, contentedly blank,
Until I hear the music, Gounod's *Mass*
For St. Cecilia, on the radio
Reminding me of Easter. I can't breathe
Against those voices, whose words I don't know,
Or with loved ones in church praying away death.
Praying my world away. I see the white explosion
Dim, the oak and pine waver and fade
From the force of that dreamy congregation.
I take my cello to the woods to serenade
The trees in their own voice, and repay
Them a soul to survive that judgment day.

3

Before we know how much we can presume
Upon the perfect pitch of compatibility,
We play to make time stand still in the room.

In our adagio ease, slow duets bloom
In afternoons that beggar hyperbole
Until we learn how little we can presume.

A nocturne together, a prize rare as a black plume:
Naked bodies tuned on the balcony over a moonlit sea
We play to make time stand still in the room.

Aubades on each other's instrument; perfume
Of honeysuckle through the window with tea,
Cheese, astonishment and plums: we presume

Such excess as ours will bring certain doom,
Obsession in winter's fevered memory,
And pray time to stand still in the room.

Harmonics on touched nerves, like strings, a loom,
Weave delirium into epiphany.
Before we know better than to presume,
We have
        played time to a standstill in our room.

4

My body can't use the logic of never
Having her again, can't credit the threat
That today and the next will be the same forever.

I torment and solace my soul with the quaver
Of my cello's lowest, most poignant string; yet
The body will hear no reason she is never

There when it thrusts against its own fever.
I can't explain to it *regret*
That this season could be the same forever.

How the wind blows in across the river.
Now our clandestine park's turned dark and wet.
What is left is immune to metaphor, may never

Sing or roar again if not to survive her:
Love imprisons me in her debt
In a year that might be the same forever.

My solo hands surge toward her absence, maneuver
My obsession to fake the chords of an old duet.
The body will hear no reason. Never.
This life and the next may be the same forever.

5

Whitman, who "broke the new wood," showed me
Where to find the trees.
The cello top is soft, resonant tone-wood
From a high stand of Engelmann spruce in Oregon,
Slow to mature in loamy soil, winged seeds, pendent cones.
For neck, sides and back, the dense Big-leaf maple,
Exotic in appearance when finished.
To make my own instrument I had to subdue
The living, rebellious wood with art, craft, and science,
Carving across its grain to form the arching, the swell
Of the cello top, whose shaping determines the instrument's
Ultimate sound.
And a "manual laborer," as Casals called himself,
Who, like the slow spruce, cared not a whit for time,
Devoting a year to learning a Bach suite,
Who showed me that age alone may not improve
The instrument, but will get better if played well.
Held between the knees, I surround it
With my own, can hear and feel that belltoned wood still
Breathing into me body to body, neck, ribs, belly, back,
Hair of the bow, grip, nut, adjusting screw,
Playing what I've made from trees, consonants, vowels,
In my own forest, on an unfretted instrument without stops
And guides, I learn the string player's habit of hearing tones
Mentally before playing them,
Playing often at the edge of an abyss of error
And worse, ignorance. But my own, free, my own.

6

I've mastered the cello for this: to fester
With music, with praise I've found no One to give.
I transcribe and play the gorgeous myths,
A pyramid for a Plumed Serpent, sacrificial
Cauldrons worked in silver, a *Pietà, Apollo,*

A glorious mosque with exquisite mirhabs at Cordoba,
Masterpieces of *Adoration* in centuries of canvas;
I practice *Requiems* and *Passions* in dumb reverence.

Yet in them lurk the Sun and Humming Bird,
Gods whose teeth ache for beating hearts;
Who are not shamed by Inquisition, Middle
Passage, Holocaust; who bless the Faithful
With the duty of war, with reward of death and Heaven.
Who leave the soloist with only his art to avert disaster.

7

For years I didn't know Helen disliked the part
I'd assigned her. She played it so well, I'd swear
Her passion was all for love, and nothing of art.

Nevertheless, there was that contralto affair.
It was so undeserved, so unbecoming,
She swore, "No more," and then took up the snare.

She'd done her best all ways to please me, humming
My romantic arrangements, never in her key,
And too slow for the tempo of her drumming.

What she prizes is dispatch and brevity,
And wants no playing before we start to play.
My cello needs skillful tuning, but she

Demurs, tone deaf to my C, G, D, and A,
Leaving me to tune my own, not knowing
What close harmonies she sends marching away

TatataDUM tatataDUM I can't keep up, slowing
Her down, retarding her pace, denying her rare
Finales with my vain cadenzas and showy bowing.

We play in adjacent, nervous spaces, a pair
Of soloists of virtuoso *ad libitum*,
Whose clashing rhythms reduce us to despair.

Her crisp, insistent flam and drag beats numb
My stuttering fingers. My arrogance now undone,
I surrender to the taDUM ta DUM taDUM DUM DUM

That underscores whatever grace we've won.
Any music at all is better than none.

V

New Poems

COUNTING THE WAYS

Heroines of opera came and gave me all
The love of their lyric hearts, whether false or true
To their tenors. Butterfly, Bess, Aida, Lulu
Reached me from the Met, La Scala, and Montreal,
Found me a small boy without a soul
And sang it into paradise. There it grew
And listened to its singing-masters imbue
It with the reverence they say a devil stole.

"I'm a woman," you came and sang me back to earth;
"I Love You," you sang paradise into bed;
"Early Autumn" consoled us for whatever fall
When you will leave and I will doubt the worth
Of all my divas, in whose voices I dread
Your voice—or the voice of no sound at all.

Sainthood

Dying is the easiest thing they have to do,
Their only way to campaign for canonization—
Accepting or seducing arrows and fire,
Abandoning the flesh and its mortal debt.

Thomas à Becket had good PR and made
Saint in three years, Assisi in only two;
Others must wait decades, centuries, to work
The required number of miracles.

Martyrs, come bring your postulators and devils'
Advocates, crowd quietly into this room
And bear witness to what I live to do:

An hour I've battled this recalcitrant child,
This relic of my flesh you see in my arms,
Before she would be rocked and sung to sleep.

Sunday, 24 May 1992, 10:30 a.m.

I hear the long, hoarse cries
Before I round the corner onto Cooper Road
And into a work in progress by the Old Master:
The young Black woman in white T-shirt, red gym pants,
Half collapsed and staggering as if from a sudden blow,
Holding her head with both hands around the implosion.
A larger woman supports her
Down the sidewalk away from the gray hearse
Backed into the gravel driveway, three men in black
Standing near, hands clasped before them, neighbors in the yard,
The front door open.
Two houses down, a Raleigh Blue & White at the curb,
The officers who have done their duty prepare to leave.
From this side of the street a woman in a uniform,
Blue cap, shirt and pants, black vest with orange stripe,
Has emerged from a car and crosses diagonally to the women
Lurching down the sidewalk toward an empty car.

I am on my walk and I walk
On, as I have planned, hearing the long hoarse cries
Awww! Awww! Awww! go back into the house
Where the dead still lies to receive them.

I know, I know. You'll be grateful you were here this morning.

In Pittsburgh, my mother rang the bell and rang the bell
For nurse, for doctor, for sons, for someone, God,
Fourteen months and twenty-four days ago, Easter Sunday.
She died before anybody came.

I: 1933–1944

My mother wanted to give me to You
while I was still a child, and we went to church.
Maybe she thought it was the only place
You could be found. I had no opinion
then, but liked the singing, and Anita Jean
would be there, sweet-smelling of Dixie Peach;
and cohorts (who droned with me through summer
days, tying strings to June bugs' legs,
and nights putting lightning bugs in Mason jars)
would be there to help bear the drone of Sunday school—
unless they belonged to the loud Baptists down the street.
The bounty of our church in Alabama
fed us, Depression-poor, whenever they harvested the steeple:
bushel baskets filled with soft bodies,
gray feathers muffling the floor, and pails of plucked
birds that memory has made small as sparrows.

The one place free of white folks, we welcomed
and abetted the visiting preacher's heresy
when he put his posters up where the deacons sat—
and showed a wooly-headed Jesus with skin
blacker than most of ours, seducing me
in one lesson into pride and skepticism.

Our dog was poisoned and died, we killed our hogs,
but there at the altar's mass of suffocating
flowers, I learned the horror of human death.
I whimpered as mourners snaked from pews to view
the corpse, whimpered as empty rows crawled closer
to where we sat, until she leaned over
sotto voce and shook me, "Child, what's the matter
with you?" And the way she always told it, my brother
Harold unsucked his thumb long enough

to pipe up, "Jerry scared of de dead man!"
She took us every Sunday, preparing us,
to get the habit, the three of us and Grandma.
I don't remember Dad—if he was there.

II: 1944–1952

Attalla to Pittsburgh, I went halfway for her,
got baptized and joined Warren Methodist Church.
I don't know where You were, but human voices
welcomed me into the choir, and the music alone
might have been the bait on the hook to catch me.
There was no hypocrisy here. My hair rose
when we sang *The Seven Last Words* at Easter,
and "Listen to the Lambs" at any time,
me pulling my chin down into my neck
to get the low notes with my adolescent bass.

From my vantage in the choir, I could see myself
in the pulpit, like both grandfathers and Dad's
brothers Moses and William. It seemed easy
to stand there and say those words, a gift
I might have, like the music and drawing skills
she gave me. There would be no surprise if one
of Aaron's sons became another Reverend Barrax.
But on a hayride to North Park, I leaped
into error, fell into sin when Juanita, the contralto
with the big tits, went with me into that October
moonlight field and let me open her blouse.
But I couldn't get past her formidable bra,
and lied when Walt asked if I had got any.

I found something to like in the church—
we had a softball team, I have a scar—
but after high school, didn't have the time.
We went on a bus trip from Warren to sing
somewhere in Washington, D.C. Even today

when I see my snapshots of our black faces
overshadowing the white ghost monuments and marble men,
I'm content to let the camera save my soul.

III: 1952–1991

She pleaded, in misdirected fear, when I went
to college, "Don't become an educated fool."

At first I resented the Holy Ghost Fathers
giving me theology instead of the philosophy
I chose as a minor—until I found
I had a taste for it, and amused myself
mocking the absurd pieties and proofs of Augustine,
Aquinas, Pascal, picking theologians'
pockets for the doctrines that suited me.

Now I went to church in books and looked
for You in physics, astronomy, myth; I compared
religions to find the least hypocritical,
the least offensive, absurd, the one whose believers
had not persecuted and murdered, one
that could survive the assault of Your greatest enemy,
the bloody Antichrist, History—
its Inquisitions, Crusades, Middle Passages,
burning crosses. Resigned, I plucked from another
book an exotic theology, and wrote in my journal,
in red, "I am a humanistic pantheist,"
satisfied at last for something to call
myself, and tried to think no more of You.

IV: March 31, 1991, Easter Sunday

A week before she died in so much pain
she didn't want to live, begging me
to come to Pittsburgh when I couldn't go,

Shani and Dara awaiting the hospital
calls to hear from me how she was: her last
words to me were for the granddaughters she loved
without measure . . . but what difference, what
difference would it have made to tell them?

God!—all those years You had Your way with me.
I gave You every chance, but when did
You bend to give me the grace, the will,
the need to believe in You? There is theology
enough to prove it's not my fault, You're to blame.
You could have listened, Lord, when she prayed for me.

To My Mother, in Heaven

Dorthera Hedrick Barrax
March 26, 1916–March 31, 1991

I'm glad they did believe it
Whom I have never found
Since the mighty Autumn afternoon
I left them in the ground.
    —Emily Dickinson, from poem 79

We didn't know we were part of history,
moving with the Black Migration
from rural South to urban North
where the jobs were, during the War.
Dad had gone before us, and I told
my friends, as best I understood,
that he worked for "Westernhouse" in Pittsburgh.
We left Attalla in 1944
to join him there, and you never saw,
never played your piano again.

You baked cakes every Christmas
and lined them up—three layers
of chocolate, lemon, coconut, caramel—
on top of the high, dull-black
upright, the only place
that kept them out of reach of Harold and me.

I'll never know how well you played
what I remember—*Moonlight Sonata,
Song of India, At Twilight*—
but it must be from the radio that I've heard
The Warsaw Concerto all these years.
The lurid sheet music for *The Burning
of Rome* was always there on the piano,
orange-yellow flames leaping

around the buildings of the imperial forum;
melodramatic as a Max Steiner
film score, you practice and practice it
all through my childhood.

It was crated and shipped to Pittsburgh for storage,
until we had room, a house, space
enough for you to have it back.
We never did. Until you divorced
ten years later, we moved
six times to rented rooms,
and only once a whole house
to ourselves, just long enough
to make you ache to have it back
before we were on someone else's
second floor again. I don't
know how long it was after
the house on Stranahan Street you gave
up, stopped paying the storage.

We bought our piano for the girls
after your last visit to Raleigh
in 1980. I was able to teach
myself to play because you'd paid
for years of violin lessons. I memorized
Moonlight Sonata for the next time you came.

I have a friend here who has a Yamaha,
what you would call a baby grand,
an ebony mirror, that would take your breath
away. I showed her the picture of you
at 32. She said you looked like a movie star.
We are both shy and self-conscious
about our playing, but feel comfortable
with each other. We play Chopin,
mostly, the *Preludes* and *Nocturnes* for you
and her father. You may know him now,
a new friend named Joshua.

If heaven is where you believed it was,
lean out, look down,
listen to us play for you.
If it's where I think it must be,
we'll make room for the two of you
on the bench here beside us.

For Barbara Baines

Trio for Two Voices and Bass Clarinet

Something takes me in its fist from chest to groin,
and so hurts my heart it forces the groan,
and extracts the tears that I can never keep;
and when its whim drops me and I can speak
again, I whisper your names, oh, from breaths so deep
that in my embarrassed, allusive streak
I confess that I have *fetched forth a sigh.*

My tone-deaf body can not identify
the modes for *lovesickness* and *mourning* by name,
and I vibrate by rote to the scores in my head
for you, sudden, new, and my mother, dead, in the same
key, requiem and rhapsody limited
to two stops, until you duet me the way
to your love, to be whole again, to joy after woe.

REUNION BIRTHDAY POEM
(WITH A LINE AFTER CUMMINGS)

We startle and laugh when the champagne bottle
Prematurely uncorks itself. Because poets
Will look for meanings everywhere, we say
It must have been a sign. But I'm afraid
Already that the old curse has found us
(When I was twenty you were still to be,
Tending your green mountains,
Rearranging the courses your rivers take to sea,
shape traveler, time shifter,
waiting for birth to get you back to me)—
Afraid we'll try and try and you will say
"But this must be wrong, Oh this must be wrong,
I shouldn't be here" and we will wither, die
(We who have hungered for each other all
Our years, whose noon has come to dine).
Instead, your eyes and mouth say O and O and O
My God, subvocal prayer that gives me back
Your twenty years to stay in you, to stay with you.

The sun at noon today at its farthest second
From earth, stops still, then slides down
Its path to shorter days, to Fall, to Winter.
Today when my life pauses and hesitates
Above your equator, you rotate your razor hips
And pubic muscles pull me back
Along the rising arc of my ecliptic.
The phantom muscle in your heart relaxes
Its grip on the pale worm, the abstract passion
Burrowed there, and we shudder in relief
When we pull it out.

I thank you, Love, for most this amazing
Day, redeemed from October when you found me
Believing myself dead, alive again
At my Solstice on Summer's sixtieth birthday.

Reunion: Our Common Language

What kind of poets have we become, to let
Love dig up our language from its ground?
Like epiphytes growing in the rain forest
Canopy, roots drawing nourishment from air
And rain, our letters rioted in italics
Of orchid desire and bromeliad magic.
The love we had abandoned all hope for, bewitched us
Out of the craft we had lived so long to learn
  "We will lean into a circle of a raging mystery
and recognize it for its secret callings . . ."
  "I'm on the verge of a cataclysm of passion with you . . ."

But naked now of your October dress
And my preacher's suit, you can't speak
Any more than I, and in our eyes
We see what simple words we lost, and why,
Standing here naked of our letters, we can not speak.

This time we have chosen perfect bodies for each other

Even though you stand with your feet together,
Sunlight, moonlight, starlight, lamplight
Shine through the space where your thighs barely touch
At the softest flesh in God's cupped hands,
Then curve into their sweet pubic hollow.
The hair there is backlit and haloed
In the pocket of light you bring
To where I kneel
Before the miniature lamps, stars, moons, novas
Shining through the cosmic arch in the middle of your body.

When we can speak with all our tongues in all our mouths,
Laughter is the word we are taught by the light,
And its sound is *prayer.*

The Old Poet Is Taken in Marriage

1

I would've bargained with any one to have loved
her first, or her alone, before I'd lived
to become a heretic of disbelief
that she has come this late, has come at all.
I despair of finding metaphor or motif
for "perfect love," nor dare even to call
it, for fear of bringing down its maudlin curse.

I tried to elevate my mumbling verse
by mimicking Emily's art, but on her stage
I declaimed to no applause under pitiless lights,
and stumbled backwards into this nonce stanza's patronage.
In the hushed immensities of our days and nights,
I stopped fretting with masks and overwrought
conceits: "Walt," I said, "look into your heart, and write."

2

The first time, like soft gongs, we are both struck
resonating to see us feel and stroke
ourselves: her spontaneous fingers ignore me
until I get voice back enough to say,
"No lover before has ever let me see,"
then honor her trust by showing her the way
my hands suppose they helped me grow from boy to man.

Now we wake from wild nights and shrink from quotidian
fears that our lost-and-found bodies and lives
may have too few years to give
before the quick scythe, or the tiny knives:
We commend our souls into our hands, live

from *I* to *Thou* in our little deaths, and teach
each other latitudes of interchangeable touch.

3

Once—no, twice—we murmured someone else's name.
You'd think we might be stricken and numb,
but we know them all, all her lovers and mine,
those who loved us well, those who did us wrong;
our Pygmalions, our tutors, our mates in Byzantine
marriage, dumb beautiful ministers, daylong
and night they accompany us to table, to bed.

For it wasn't "*Oh, Jesus!*" then, but Oh Fred
who made her swoon for dildoes (our "Lost Boys"
now); Jenny, whose carrot-stick rhythms drove me mad.
They bring us more than the sum of buzzing toys
and erection rings, these carnal ghosts of our myriad
couplings. Confessing to them was the test
we passed to bank our souls in mutual trust.

4

Every time Emily disappears on stage,
she decoys dim-witted death from his siege,
losing her in Hedda, Cordelia, Antigone.
His baffled fingers miscalculate her years,
and she seems never to age.
                                            Not so with me.
My ostentatious love provokes his jeers
and impatience to disassemble my molecules,
to scatter me among his love-sick fools—
no more than I deserve for unholy sonnets.
Even as she mourned me, the rigors of her art
would still demand rehearsals for her Juliets,

her Stellas. It won't matter then if my part
is taken by a raw Romeo (she'll age him);
but tonight I'm here when Desdemona comes home.

5

Poets who swagger and strut make me sick
with envy, even when they pout and suck
their teeth if you question their genius, or worse,
ignore them. And I envy the arrogance
that lets them bluster through their cutpurse
verses—untroubled, cocksure, smug sycophants
of fame—while yet I marvel, in terrified humility,
that poems come to me at all, as Emily
did, for no reason I can understand.
I woke today after we had slept so still,
her arm across my hip, held all night in her hand,
and thought I still slept and dreamed, until
her drowsy fingers squeezed me back from disbelief
that I haven't stolen someone else's life.

Perfect Stranger

I left her in Performing Arts for Science Fiction
and my heart, breath and feet all
stumbled when my mind idled
around a corner down an aisle
and in a distant moment my fuzzy eye
misperceived her through its protein waterfall
mist as a perfect stranger.

It's happened a hundred times before: the little moan
that such a woman would never have
the likes of me, crazed by the shadow drama
of her unknowable life, taunted by that
lover in my place, the pledge of all I own,
or one year, for "just one night"—what more
can one give that's his alone?

Instead of a year lopped off my life,
l have twenty-three for Emily, rescued
from smoking.
                    She turns and sees my foolish face
and smiles that frown I know from memory.
When I get to her
she looks behind the cataracts I can't keep
from my eyes and asks, "What is it?"
with hands where no stranger can ever touch me.

THE GUILT

He made himself her compost heap, and hoped
Something old or something new would grow
Where he kept the guilt always in the best light
For her tending, fertilized with bile and bonemeal
Ashes shaken through the grate in his heart.
She used her privilege of a good woman done wrong
And opened him up at will to nurse and prune
It, until the habit of their make-do lives
One day lulled them offguard into a casual quarrel,
And she turned at bay with her cri de coeur,
"I will never forgive you, never." He set his face
To muffle its shout of deliverance
When his seahorse womb aborted the misshapen thing
And, midwife to himself, he became a something new.

Jeopardy

How little it takes to break a heart:
In my Winn-Dixie cart, I had the new Fudge Brownie flavor
of Healthy Choice Low Fat Premium Ice Cream;
I had Almaden, Bounty, Canada Dry, Charmin Plus;
I had CoffeeMate and Glade Plug In—
no more than I needed for the express line,
fast-walking past a woman haranguing her four
to stay put at the end of the aisle—
a lovely group portrait of elder daughter and son,
two smaller boys, all brightly neat and starched,
the Black family we'd all like to see,
who seemed there must be a father for.
She harried herself back to the shelf
for the bypassed peanut butter,
proudly assuring them that one more
would drive her crazy.
But I wasn't walking fast enough
and heard the slap
of fingers on knuckles
breaking them apart, and
"Little boys don't hold hands!"

I lurched to
a stop
and turned in time
to see the brothers
four and six
side by side in each other's ruin
looking up in perfect trust
at their mother.

Indecisive and cowardly, I let her get away.

In Their Heaven

Won't there be lovely, hideous yowls
when the risen discover on Judgment Day
with God and the Devil sitting at each other's right hand
that there had been a scribal error
by a first-century monk with strabismus
(Brother Salducci) who got the colors wrong?

When they bow before the throne of snow-white radiance,
they will rise into Satan's beatific smile.

PITTSBURGH, 1948: THE MUSIC TEACHER

I don't know where my mother got him—
whose caricature he was—or how
he found me, to travel by streetcars
on Saturday mornings to the Negro
home, our two rooms and bath on the Hornsby's
second floor. His name was Professor
Something-or-Other Slavic, portly,
florid man, bald pate surrounded
by stringy gray hair. Everything
about him was threadbare: wing collar,
string tie, French cuffs, cut-away coat.
His sausage fingers were grimy, his nails
dirty. I think, now, he was one of the War's
Displaced Persons, who accepted with grace
coming to give violin lessons
to a 15-year-old alien boy
(displaced here myself from a continent,
from a country I couldn't name,
and a defector from Alabama).
I was the debt he had to pay
on the short end of a Refugee's desperate
wager, or prayer, to redeem the body
before the soul. I don't know why
my mother didn't give him
his paltry three dollars. I had to do it.

One morning he stood
at my side waving his bow
in time to my playing, swayed
once and crumpled to the kitchen
floor that she had made
spotless for him, taking
the music stand down.
I stood terrified until she
ran in and we helped him to his feet.

He finished my lesson in dignified shame,
and I knew, from pure intuition,
he had not eluded the hounds of hunger.

Outside of death camps I'd seen liberated
in newsreels and *Life*, it was the first time, I think,
I'd felt sorry for anyone white.

SURREAL DREAMS: AFTER WATCHING
THE DISCOVERY CHANNEL

I see buildings counterfeit trees and sky in their windows for birds
to fly into clouds like drift nets wide as the continent
played out from their ships by Viking and samurai whalers
they sweep the ocean and kill all they catch
krill shrimp tuna frigate seahorse albatross grouper starfish eel man-of-war
in drift nets wide as the continent
fish with birds exhausted from migration in their stomachs
there is the Sea Shepherd sailing with the white warrior from Wounded Knee
to free buffalo and blue whale from drift nets
wide as the continent
but still virgin dolphins swim to the altar where Lord Shiva
and his brides
the orca nuns
wait with harpoons hidden under their habits
        "Your ships, Captains, why are your ships
        outfitted for transporting whales and trying blacks?" Well,
Dear reader, you sucker, you gull, you goat,
Did you shake your head in wonder that my Images
Are so Deep and dreamy, my Realism so Sur,
My consciousness so streamy? You wouldn't think,
Would you, I'd waste your time or mine, or betray the trust
You have in poets, that I didn't have a Truth in slant
To tell you—unless you believe McLeish's sly subversion
That "a poem must not mean but be"? Well, you chump,
Why should a stranger's dream mean anything to you?
I tried to warn you with that stupid title—
But you see "dream" and think "surreal" and it could mean
Anything or nothing at all, more fraud than Freud.
(I hope you admire the Shiva and orca thing,
and those clever phallic harpoons!)
So listen, you sap, this was no dream, for I lay broad waking
When I made up this crap and had no more significance in mind
Than you'd find in a rap, and the next time you see a dream poem

You should turn the page or you may be screwed again
But by someone less honest than me.
But it was so good, it felt so good to do this to you.
But then, you know, I may be lying. We do that.

HANDS OFF

I don't want to seem a bigot—
or worse, uncivil—but hesitate
to shake their hands. Grandmothers (nurses),
our mothers, aunts, and sisters (maids)
have come home from inside their secrets,
generations infiltrating their camps
(before much was known about
E. coli or hepatitis A),
and warned us about their "nasty habits."
Many have been my friends, I've loved
a few, followed them into bathrooms,
and found soap still dry.
Thus this paranoia of hands—
like those on the guy in the next stall,
or shaking his limp, pissy dick
at the urinal.
              They just walk out.

HELEN AND THE ANIMALS

We curse them with terrifying, hybrid names
Like wolf spider, tiger beetle, ghost crab,
Then grumble when they don't settle our claims
And define which symbol to favor: Adam or Ahab.
They have no brains to speak of, no hands to fire
Up for cooking, no cutlery for neat
Dining. I find it easy to admire
The immaculate will conferred to kill and eat
Their kind. But not Helen. She deplores
The kindergarten irony that she
Is "a great consumer of meat," but abhors
Hyenas, who keep the Serengeti free
Of plagues. The only kingdoms left are theirs
And God's, neither ennobled by human heirs.

No Answers

How is it that those charming connubial pairs
Of pagan gods, and their offspring, have disappeared?
Where are they now, when there are no more prayers
Or sacrifices to them, beloved and feared?
How is it that Zeus and Hera, Odin and Frigg,
And lonely Atum-Ra, whose wife was his hand,
Would suffer their own creatures to renege
On their worship, and send them packing off to Lotus-land?
If believed once, then they still must exist;
If not now, they never had been real:
This logic haunts me most when you insist
That outside your faith, your path, there's no appeal
To any heaven; a theology so odd
Should shame its subject into replacing itself as God.